THE LIFE OF DAVID

THE MAN AFTER
GOD'S OWN HEART

THE
LIFE
OF
DAVID

F.B. MEYER

Edited for Today's Reader by
LANCE WUBBELS

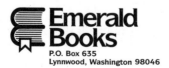

P.O. Box 635
Lynnwood, Washington 98046

Scripture quotations are taken from the King James Version of the Bible.

The Life of David

Copyright © 1995
Lance C. Wubbels

All Rights Reserved.

ISBN 1-883002-21-4

Published by Emerald Books
P.O. Box 635
Lynnwood, Washington 98046

Printed in the United States of America.

PREFACE

*T*he character and life of David are supremely fascinating, not only to holy souls who find their deepest thoughts expressed in his unrivaled psalms but also to all men. David's life and character exhibit a humanness, a variety, a sharp contrast in experiences, and traits of generosity and courage that always elicit admiration.

While sketching every period of David's life, I have concentrated on those sections of Scripture that trace the steps by which the shepherd became the king. These were the steps through which David's character was formed, his sweetest psalms composed, and those manifold experiences encountered that enabled David to interpret and utter the universal heart of man.

David was the sweet singer of the world, the ancestor of Christ, and the founder of a dynasty of kings. He was a prophet, as the apostle Peter tells us (Acts 2:30), inspired and taught by the Holy Ghost. As a type and forerunner of Him who, though his Son, was also his Lord, David was also the man after God's own heart who "did that which was right in the eyes of the Lord and turned not aside from any thing that he commanded him all the days of his life, save only in the matter of Uriah the Hittite" (1 Kings 15:5). As long as time remains, David will always enlist our affection and command our respect.

F.B. Meyer

About The Editor

LANCE WUBBELS, the Managing Editor of Bethany House Publishers, taught biblical studies courses at Bethany College of Missions for many years. he is also the author of *The Gentle Hills* fiction series and a heartwarming short novel, *One Small Miracle*, with Bethany House.

As the compiler and editor of the Charles Spurgeon and F.B. Meyer Christian Living Classic books, Wubbels' desire is to present these classic writings in a way that will appeal to a wide audience of readers and allow their timeless messages to be as relevant today as the day they were penned. The writings of both Spurgeon and Meyer are filled with practical insight that will enrich believers' lives.

Contents

INTRODUCTION

For over a century, the writings of F.B. Meyer have provided Christians with a treasure trove of lasting value, affirming the truths of the gospel for every age. Crowning a life of worldwide ministry by voice and pen, Meyer's books reflect a depth of spiritual experience and singlemindedness of vision that one rarely finds in contemporary writing. It is for this reason that Lance Wubbels has chosen to edit and update this remarkable biography of one of God's greatest biblical saints.

F.B. Meyer wrote twelve portraits of the giants of the Old and New Testaments. These detailed, inspirational biographies are filled with insight, challenge, and comfort. It is comforting to find that these great figures were not so different from ourselves—sometimes weak, indifferent, willful. Yet they had their moments of faith, humility, and courage, and God was able to use these for His greater purposes. God's faithfulness, which not only accepts but transforms such inconsistency, calls us to more effective Christian living.

It cannot be stressed enough that these are thoroughly biblical portraits. It is essential that the scripture listed at the beginning of each chapter be read first. Meyer's wrote the chapter with it firmly in his mind that the reader would have his Bible opened to that scripture and be completely familiar with its context. Attempting to read the chapter without studying the listed scripture will leave the reader in the dark at some points. The editor gives his strongest recommendation that you first read the scripture and then follow along as Meyer develops his thoughts based upon the biblical text.

You are invited to read these powerful chapters as you would listen to a trusted and skilled pastor. There is nothing speculative about Meyer's teaching. He will meet you where you live in an understandable manner that inspires and challenges, and you will not be disappointed. Life-changing messages await your reading.

Careful editing has helped to sharpen the focus of these messages and update the language while retaining the authentic and timeless flavor they undoubtedly bring.

1

1 Samuel 16:1

CALLED AS A SHEPHERD

We stride the river daily at its spring,
Nor in our childish thoughtlessness foresee
What myriad vassal streams shall tribute bring,
How like an equal it shall greet the sea.

O small beginnings! Ye are great and strong,
Based on a faithful heart and weariless brain;
Ye build the future fair, ye conquer wrong,
Ye earn the crown, and wear it not in vain.

J.R. Lowell

*T*he story of David opens with a dramatic contrast between the fresh hope of David's young life and the rejection of the self-willed King Saul, whose course was rapidly descending toward the fatal field of Gilboa.

Few have had a fairer chance than Saul. Richly gifted, handsome and tall, favored by nature and opportunity, Saul might have made one of the greatest names in history. His first exploit, the relief of Jabesh-gilead, justified the wildest anticipations of his friends. But the fair dawn was soon overcast. The hot impatience that persisted in offering the sacrifice before Samuel came, his needless oath and ruthless proposal to take Jonathan's life, his flagrant disobedience to the distinct charge respecting Amalek—all proved that he was not fit to act as God's representative and that he must be set aside.

9

The final announcement of Saul's removal from office was made at Gilgal. It was at that spot that the nation of Israel obeyed Joshua's command and rolled away the reproach of uncircumcision when they entered Canaan. Gilgal suggested humility as the only condition on which God can use human instruments. But in Saul's case, there had been no humbling of pride, no submission of self-will, no putting away of the wild energy of the flesh. Saul was called while seeking his father's straying asses, in contrast to David, who was called while watching his father's sheep, and there was a good deal of the wild-ass nature about Saul that reminds one of Ishmael, which nature neither of them sought to subdue. Saul rejected the word of the Lord, and the Lord rejected Saul from being king (1 Samuel 15:23).

From Gilgal, Saul went up to his house at Gibeah in the heights of Benjamin. Samuel went to his house at Ramah, a little to the south. Samuel had judged Israel from Ramah for twenty years—and there he dwelt as a father and a priest among the people, known far and near as the man of God (1 Samuel 7:17; 9:6–12). It was there that he also mourned for Saul. No bad man drifts down the rapids unwarned or unwept, but the divine purpose cannot wait until such pitying tears are dried. Nor must we cling to the grave of the dead beyond the time when the Spirit of God has moved on. We must arise to follow as God transfers the focus of His operation from the rocky heights of Benjamin to the breezy uplands of Bethlehem and conducts us to the house of Jesse.

In the selection of every man for high office in the service of God and man, there are two sides: the divine and the human. The election of God is followed by its elaboration in history. There is the heavenly summons, and the earthly answer to its ringing notes. We must therefore consider the root of David in God, the stem of Jesse (that is, the local circumstances that might account for what the boy was), and the white bud of a noble life.

The Root Of David

The prophecy of Isaiah (11:10) refers to a root of Jesse (David's father), and twice in the book of Revelation, our Lord is called the Root of David:

> The Lion of the tribe of Juda, the Root of David, hath prevailed to open the book, and to loose the seven seals thereof (Revelation 5:5).

10

And still more emphatically we find among the last words spoken by the Savior before the curtain of the ages fell:

> I Jesus...am the root and the offspring of David, and the bright and the morning star (Revelation 22:16).

The idea suggested is of an old root, hidden deep in the earth, that sends up its green scions and sturdy stems. David's character may be considered as an emanation from the life of the Son of God before He took upon Himself the nature of man, as well as an anticipation of what Jesus was to be and do in the fullness of time. Jesus was the Son of David, yet in another sense He was David's ancestor. Thus, we return to the ancient puzzle that Jesus of Nazareth is at once David's Lord and Son (Mark 12:35–37).

There are four great biblical phrases about the choice of David, and the last phrase strikes deeply into the heart of that great mystery.

The Lord hath sought Him a man (1 Samuel 13:14). No one can know the day or hour when God passes by, seeking for precious vessels and beautiful pearls. When we least expect it, we are being scrutinized, watched, and tested in the daily commonplaces to see whether we will be faithful in more momentous issues. Let us be always on the alert, our armor in place, our lamps burning, our nets mended and cleansed.

I have found David My servant (Psalm 89:20). There is ecstacy in that voice, like that of the shepherd who *found* the lost sheep in Luke 15. David was found long before Samuel sent for him. When was the moment of that blessed discovery? Was it one dawn, when in the first flicker of daylight the young shepherd led his flock from fold to pasture? Or was it one morning, when in an outburst of heroic faith he rescued a trembling lamb from lion or bear? Or was it one afternoon, when the first conception of the shepherd psalm stirred in his heart as he sat and watched his charge? Or was it one night, when David heard the silent speech of the heavens declaring the glory of God? And was there not some secret glad response to the Master's call, like that which the disciples gave when Jesus found them at the nets and said, "Follow me"?

He chose David also His servant (Psalm 78:70). The people chose Saul, but God chose David. This made David strong. He was conscious that the purpose of God lay behind and beneath him.

When, in the years that followed, Saul drove David into hiding or Michael taunted him about his extravagant gestures, the thought that he was divinely commissioned was David's standby (2 Samuel 7:21). We are immovable when we touch the bedrock of God's choice and hear Him say, "He is a chosen vessel unto me, to bear my name" (Acts 9:15).

The Lord hath commanded him to be captain over His people (1 Samuel 13:14). Appointments are not solely due to human patronage or won by human effort; they are of God. *He* brings low and lifts up. Saul might chafe and fret, but from amidst the ruins of Saul's waning power, the authority of David emerged like a sun from a pillar of clouds because God willed it. Equip yourself for God's service and be faithful. God will appoint you in His time, and you will know that the promotion comes neither from the east nor from the west but comes from above.

I have provided Me a king (1 Samuel 16:1). That answers everything. The divine provision meets every need and silences every anxiety. Let us not yield to anxieties about the future of the Church or for our nation. God has provided against all contingencies. In some unlikely place—perhaps a shepherd's hut or a humble cottage—God has His prepared and appointed instrument. As yet the shaft is hidden in His quiver, in the shadow of His hand; but at the precise moment when it will accomplish its greatest effect, it will be produced and launched in the air.

THE STEM OF JESSE

We turn for a moment to consider the formative influences of David's young life. The family dwelt on the ancestral property where Boaz, that mighty man of wealth, had brought the Rose fo Moab. Perhaps it was somewhat decayed through the enforced taxation of the Philistine garrison that seems to have been posted in the little town. We read of the *few* sheep in the wilderness that composed the flock and that the present sent by Jesse to his soldier sons was meager in extreme. The conditions under which Jesse raised his large family of eight sons and two daughters were probably hard enough to severly tax the endurance and industry of them all.

David says nothing of his father, but twice speaks of his mother as "the handmaid of the Lord." From her David derived his poetic gift, his sensitive nature, his deeply spiritual character. To his father,

David was the lad who kept the sheep, who was not worthy to be summoned to the religious feast. To his mother, he was David the beloved, and she probably was the first to hear the psalms that have charmed and soothed the world. David honored them both with dutiful service, and when it seemed possible they might suffer serious harm because of their relationship to him, amid the pelting storm of Saul's persecution, David removed his parents to the safe-keeping of the king of Moab in the land of his ancestress.

The lad may have also owed something to the schools of the prophets that were established by Samuel's wise prescience to maintain the knowledge of the law of Israel (1 Samuel 19:20). They in every instance appear to have been richly endued with the gracious power of the Holy Ghost. The company of the prophets would undoubtedly visit Bethlehem and find an eager response in the guileless nature of the young shepherd. From them David would learn to reduce his melodies to metrical order and to accompany them with the harp. And from them, too, David learned to know and prize the divine Word.

But nature was his nurse, his companion, and his teacher. Bethlehem is situated six miles to the south of Jerusalem by the main road leading to Hebron. Its site is two thousand feet above the level of the Mediterranean, on the northeast slope of the long gray ridge, with a deep valley on either side. These valleys unite at a short distance to the east and run down toward the Dead Sea. On the gentle slopes of the hills the fig, olive, and vine grow luxuriantly. In the valleys are the rich cornfields, where Ruth once gleaned and that gave the place its name, "the House of Bread." The moorlands around Bethlehem, forming the greater part of the Judean plateau, do not, however, present features of soft beauty but are wild, gaunt, strong—places that build character. There shepherds have always led and watched their flocks, and there David first imbibed that knowledge of natural scenery and of pastoral pursuits that colored the rest of his life and poetry.

Such were the schools and schoolmasters of David's youth. But preeminently, David's spirit lay open to the Spirit of God, who brooded over David's young life—teaching, quickening, and ennobling him, opening to him the books of nature and revelation, and pervading his heart with such an innocent trust as the dumb sheep of his charge reposed in him. In the spiritual as in the physical realm, David had every reason to say long after, "My substance was not hid from thee, when I was made in secret, and curiously wrought in the lowest parts of the earth" (Psalm 139:15).

THE WHITE BUD OF A NOBLE LIFE

Although David did not have the splendid physique of his brother Eliab, who so impressed the aged Samuel, he was strong and athletic. His feet were nimble as a gazelle's, he could leap a wall or outstrip a troop, a bow of steel could be easily broken by his young arms, and a stone sent from his sling would hit the mark with unerring precision. Too slight to wear a man's armor, yet he was able to rend a lion or a bear. His face glowed with health. The blue of his eyes and beauty of his fair complexion were in strong contrast to the darker countenances of his companions. The sensitiveness of the poet's soul was combined with daring, resource, and a power to command. His dress was a coarse and simple tunic; his equipment was a sling, a rod, and a staff.

David's soul is reflected in many psalms that must be attributed to this period of his life because they are so free from the pressure of sorrow and anxiety. Among these psalms are the eighth, nineteenth, twenty-third, and twenty-ninth. They are so full of wonder that Jehovah should care for man and yet so confident that He was his shepherd. David was deeply stirred by the aspect of the heavens and yet convinced that the words of God were equally divine. He was afraid of secret faults and presumptuous sins. He was anxious to join in the universal chorus of praise, ascending from the orchestra of nature, yet he was certain that there were yearnings and faculties within his soul that nature could not participate in and that made him nature's high priest and chorister. We will visit these again—they are too radiant with a light that never shone on sea or shore for us to pass them so lightly by.

Ah, guileless, blessed boy! You could not know that you would die amid the blare of trumpets announcing the accession to the throne of your son, the splendid Solomon. Still less could you dream that your unsullied nature would one day be befouled by so sad a stain! Yet your God loves you, and you will teach us many lessons as we turn the pages of your wonderful career—poet, minstrel, soldier, exile, king—and read them in the light that streams from the face of your greatest Son, who was born of the seed of David according to the flesh but was declared to be the Son of God by the resurrection of the dead!

2

1 Samuel 16:13

FROM THAT
DAY FORWARD

Once for the least of children of Monasses
God had a message and a deed to do,
Wherefore the welcome that all speech surpasses
Called him and hailed him greater than he knew.

F.W.H. Myers

*F*rom whatever angle we study the life of David, it is remarkable. It may be that Abraham excelled him in faith, and Moses in the power of concentrated fellowship with God, and Elijah in the fiery force of his enthusiasm. But none of these was so multifaceted as the richly gifted son of Jesse.

Few have had so varied a career as David—a shepherd and monarch, poet and soldier, champion of his people and outlaw in the caves of Judea, beloved of Jonathan and persecuted by Saul, vanquishing the Philistines one day and accompanying them into battle on another. But in every venture he seemed to possess a special power with God and man that could not be accounted for by the fascination of his manner, the beauty of his features, the rare gifts with which his nature was endowed, or the spiritual power that was so remarkable an attribute of his heart. We touch these many chords, but the secret still eludes us, until we read the momentous words that sum up the result of a memorable day that lay as a jewel in the obscure years of David's youth: "The Spirit of the LORD came upon David from that day forward" (1 Samuel 16:13).

IT BEGAN LIKE ANY ORDINARY DAY

No angel trumpet heralded this day. No faces looked out of heaven. The sun arose that morning according to its custom over the purple walls of the hills of Moab, making the cloud curtains saffron and gold. With the first glimmer of light, the boy was on his way to lead his flock to pasturelands heavy with dew. As the morning hours sped onward, many duties concerning the sheep would occupy his watchful soul—strengthening the weak, healing the sick, binding up the broken, and seeking the lost. If he was not busy, the music of his song may have thrilled the listening air, for "a cunning player on the harp" was he (1 Samuel 16:16).

A breathless messenger suddenly broke upon this pastoral scene with the tidings of Samuel's arrival at the little town and announcing that the prophet had refused to eat of the hastily prepared banquet until the shepherd boy had joined the guests. David's father had therefore sent the messenger to summon David with all speed. How the young eyes must have flashed with pleasure! David had never before been wanted and sent for like this. Until now, he had been only "the youngest and, behold, he keepeth the sheep" (1 Samuel 16:11). The family life had been complete without him. His father and brothers had followed their pursuits and pleasures in almost total disregard of the young son and brother who was destined to make their names immortal. David had borne it all in patience. His heart was not proud; neither were his eyes lofty. David did not exercise himself in great matters or in things too high for him, but he quieted himself as a child who is weaned from its mother. Still, it was a genuine pleasure for David to feel that the family circle in great Samuel's eyes was not complete until he had come. David therefore left his sheep with the messenger and started at full speed for home.

With his arrival, Samuel had sanctified Jesse and his sons, passing them through a series of ceremonial ablutions to fit them for the festival in which the social and sacred elements combined. But

David needed none of these. His pure and guiltless soul was right with God and clothed in the spotless robe of purity. No dirt needed scrupulous removal. Let us so live as to be prepared for whatever the next hour may bring. Let us keep our spirit in fellowship with God and our robe sinlessly pure. The faithful fulfillment of the commonplaces of daily life is the best preparation for any great demand that may suddenly break in upon our lives.

IT WAS THE CONSUMMATION OF PREVIOUS TRAINING

We must not suppose that this was the first time that the Spirit of God worked in David's heart. To think this would indicate a complete misconception of the special teaching of this incident, for Scripture always distinguishes between the regenerating and the anointing grace of the Holy Spirit. From his earliest days, David had probably been the subject of a divine quickening and renewing work. But before this day, David had probably never experienced the special empowering of the Holy One that was symbolized in the anointing oil, an anointing indispensable for all successful spiritual work.

Our Lord Jesus was born of the Spirit, but His anointing for service did not take place until the age of thirty when He emerged from the waters of John's baptism. It was to this Jesus referred in the opening words of His earliest sermon, "The Spirit of the Lord is upon me, and he hath anointed me" (Luke 4:18). The apostles were certainly regenerate before the day of Pentecost, but they had to wait within closed doors until they were endued with power from on high for the conversion of men. We have met many who were unmistakably the children of God but who had no special power in witnessing, no freedom in their speech, no ability to grapple with the hearts and consciences of men. Spiritually, they needed what would be to them as electricity to the wire or the spark to gunpowder. In other words, the Spirit of God has been *in* but not *on* them. We have seen such believers awake and claim the divine anointing, and suddenly they have begun to speak with new tongues, and men have not been able to resist their reasonings of sin, righteousness, and judgment to come.

This blessed anointing for service cannot be ours unless there has been a previous gracious work on the heart. There must be the new life—the life of God. There must be submission of heart, humility, faithfulness to duty, cleansing from known sin, and a close walk with God. The descending flame must fall upon the whole burnt offering of a consecrated life. And it was because all these had been accomplished in David by the previous work of the Holy Spirit that David was prepared for this special empowering. It may be that in the obscurity of your life, shut away from the presence of great matters, you are being prepared for a similar experience. Be careful to obey God's smallest prompting so that you may be prepared for the golden moment when your meek head shall be suddenly bathed in the descending anointing.

IT WAS MINISTERED THROUGH SAMUEL

The old prophet had conferred many benefits on his native land, but none could compare in importance with his eager care for its youth. The creation of the schools of the prophets was due to him. Saul, in the earlier years of his manhood, felt the charm and spell of the old man's character. The stalwart sons of Jesse's house were therefore probably well known to Samuel when he received the divine command to anoint one of them as Saul's successor.

Driving a heifer before him, Samuel entered the one long street of Bethlehem and summoned the elders to a feast so as not to arouse the suspicions of the jealous, moody king. Saul would not have been reluctant to take Samuel's life had he suspected the real object of the prophet's visit.

When David reached the village, a strange scene met his eye. There was his father Jesse and his seven brothers, probably waiting for him in the ancestral home, preparatory to their all going together to the public banquet to which the leading men of the village had been invited. An unusual restraint lay upon the rough tongues and harsh behavior with which Eliab and the others were used to treating David. At other times, they would not have hesitated to express their impatience and contempt, but now the very air seemed heavy with a sacred spell that held them. No sooner had David entered, flushed with exertion, health glowing on his face, genius flashing from his eye, royalty in his appearance, than the Lord said to Samuel, "Arise, anoint him: for this is he!" (1 Samuel 16:12). Then Samuel took the horn of oil that he had brought with him from Nob and poured its contents on the head of the astonished lad.

It is likely that the bystanders did not realize the significance of that act. Had they, Jesse would not have treated David so unceremoniously on the eve of the fight with Goliath, and Eliab would have addressed him with more courtesy. But David probably understood. The Jewish historian Josephus indeed tells us that the prophet whispered in David's ear the meaning of the sacred symbol. Did the aged lips approach the young head and, as the trembling hand pushed back the clustering locks, whisper in the lad's ear the thrilling words, "You shall be king"? If so, in the days that followed, how those words would return to David and how vast an inspiration they would be! Samuel's words would be a formative influence, a preparation for the great destiny that awaited David.

The descent of the oil was symbolic; in other words, it had no spiritual power but was the outward and visible sign that the Spirit of God had come mightily on the shepherd lad. For Jesus there was no oil, but rather, the appearance of a dove flitting gently to its nest. For the disciples on the day of Pentecost there was no oil, but a flame of glowing fire alighting on each bowed head. Over time, these outward symbols have become mechanical and have passed from general use. We must believe that we have received when we have fulfilled the conditions of humility and the faith that claims (Galatians 3:14).

From that memorable day, David returned to his sheep. As the months went slowly by, he must have sometimes greatly wondered when the hour of achievement would arrive. When would he have an opportunity to display and use his newfound force? He had to learn that we are sometimes strengthened with all power through patience and longsuffering as the prelude to heroic deeds. We have to wrestle with the lion and the bear on the hills of Bethlehem, that we may be prepared to meet Goliath in the valley of Elah.

IT WAS A DAY OF REJECTION

Seven of Jesse's sons were passed over. Not many wise men after the flesh, not many mighty, not many noble were called. God chose then, as always, the weak, the base, the things that were despised. Seven is the number of perfection, and I take it that the seven sons of Jesse stand for the perfection of the flesh. This must be cut down to the ground lest it should glory in God's presence. The lesson is hard to learn, but its acquisition is imperative. You say you cannot bear it? Well, be it so. Then, like Eliab, you may become one of the princes of Judah, but you shall never be God's beloved (1 Chronicles 27:18).

In this secret anointing of David—the first of three—we have a type of the setting apart of our Lord in the divine counsels. Rejected of men, despised of His brethren, without form or beauty, Jesus has been set apart as the King of the Ages. As yet many a barrier lies between Him and the acknowledgment that the Father has promised); but to Him every knee shall bow and every tongue shall confess that He is Lord (Philippians 2:10-11). In the meanwhile, He waits till the hour of universal triumph strikes. Jesus Christ waits till the many crowns of the destined empire meet on the head that was once encircled by the crown of thorns.

3

1 Samuel 16:18–19

SUMMONED TO THE PALACE

He bowed himself
With all obedience to the king, and wrought
All kind of service with a noble ease,
That graced the lowliest act in doing of it.

Tennyson

Some have supposed that the incident we are now to consider belongs to a subsequent page in David's history, following the narrative of the slaying of Goliath so as to make that the occasion of the young shepherd's introduction to Saul. This transposition seems to be called for by Saul's slowness to recognize his former minstrel in the young warrior who stood before him with the head of the Philistines' champion in his hand.

This lack of recognition may be accounted for by David's growth as a man between the period of his being a minstrel and his first great exploit in the battlefield. How long that interval lasted we cannot tell, but during its course, David had grown from youth to manhood, his physique become stalwart and robust, his face molded by the growing soul within. If we reject this explanation and do not allow the incident to remain where we find it, we have to face the additional difficulty of how Saul's courtiers could dare to introduce to their master one whose successes had already stirred this jealousy (1 Samuel 18:8–9). We would also have to explain why it was necessary to give so many details in describing the personality of the young singer (1 Samuel 16:18). Surely it would have been sufficient to recall what David had done in the vale of Elah to identify him at once. We hold, therefore, that this story should stand in the place it has held ever since this narrative was penned.

After his anointing, David returned to his sheep. When Saul, who was advised by his courtiers, sent for David to charm away his depression, this was the specific indication he gave to Jesse: "Send me David, thy son, which is with the sheep" (1 Samuel 16:19). It says a great deal for the simplicity and ingenuousness of the boy's character that he would have returned to the fold to lead and guard his helpless charge, faithfully fulfilling the routine of daily duty while waiting for God to do what Samuel had spoken. Similarly, Jesus left the temple, where to His boyish eyes a radiant glimpse had been afforded of doing His Father's business, and returned home to be subject to the carpenter's shop.

A contemporary of David has given a brief portrait of David's character as it presented itself during this period to casual observers. One of Saul's young men said, "Behold, I have seen a son of Jesse the Beth-lehemite, that is cunning in playing, and a mighty valiant man, and a man of war, and prudent in matters, and a comely person, and the LORD is with him" (1 Samuel 16:18). These five characteristics enable us to form a graphic conception of the young hero who was making the countryside ring with his renown.

THE MINSTREL

David had the temperament of a poet, being sensitive to nature and open to every impression from mountain and vale, from dawn to evening. And he also had the power of translating his impressions into speech and song. His psalms are read with devotion to the present day and will as long as man shall live. Who can forget the story of the green strips of meadowland where his flocks grazed at noon, or the little stream somewhere near Bethlehem of whose peaceful waters they drank, or the smooth paths that he selected for their feet, or the rocky gorge where they were in danger of lion and bear?

A modern poet loves to imagine David reciting his verses, singing to the tune of his harp, calling to his sheep. We love to think of David's reflections on the song of the autumn harvest, the joyous marriage poem, the solemn funeral dirge, the chant of the Levites as they performed their sacred duties, the marching music of the men of Bethlehem when they repelled some border raid. And we might add to these David's marvelous power in depicting the sacred hush of dawn, where there is neither speech nor language, just before the sun leaps up as a bridegroom to run his race, and the solemn pomp of night, where worlds beyond worlds open to the wondering gaze. And to these we might add the marvelous description of the thunderstorms that broke over Palestine, rolling peal after peal, from the great waters of the Mediterranean, over the cedars of Lebanon to the far distant wilderness of Kadesh, until the sevenfold thunders are followed by torrents of rain and these by the clear shining in which Jehovah blesses His people with peace (Psalms 23; 19; 8; 29).

The psalm began with David. Its lyric beauty and tender grace, its rhythmic measure, its exuberant hallelujahs and plaintive lamentations, its inimitable expression of the changeful play of light and shade over the soul, its blending of nature and godliness, its references to the life of men and the world as regarded from the standpoint of God—these elements in the psalter that have endeared it to holy souls in every age owe their origin to the poetic, heaventouched soul of the sweet singer of Israel. Little wonder that Saul's young man said that David was cunning in playing! The psalms that David composed in those early days—which are so delightfully free from the darker elements that persecution and unkindness and consciousness of sin introduced into the later creation of his genius—were destined to go singing throughout the world and time, working on men the same effects that they wrought on the king, of whom it is said that when David took the harp and played with his hand, Saul was refreshed.

THE YOUNG WARRIOR

There was abundant opportunity for the education of David's dexterity and daring. The Philistines' frontier was not far from his native town. It is probable that there were many repetitions of the incident of later years, when the Philistines held the well of Bethlehem and placed a guard demanding toll of the water. Many a skirmish had the men of Bethlehem with the border warriors, who would sweep down upon the produce of their vineyards and corn-fields when the harvest was ripe. In these David acquired the character of being a man of valor and a mighty man of war. It may be that sometimes he had to stand alone against a handful of sheep stealers intent on plundering the fold.

David tells us how he needed to be on the alert against the wild beasts that prowled the hills of Judah—the lion with his hungry teeth, the bear with his deadly hug. For these David had no fear. He smote them and delivered the trembling lambs from their mouth. He caught them by their beard and slew them. He could break a bow of steel with those strong young arms and wield Goliath's sword with ease. He could club a wild beast with his staff and hurl a stone with unerring aim. David was a proud young Samson, laughing in the fullness of his manly strength.

But David would have been the last to attribute his exploits to his physical strength. By faith he had learned to avail himself of the power of God. Was David not God's servant, designated for a great mission, summoned to wage uncompromising war with the uncircumcised? David might be a babe, yet out of his mouth God had established strength in order to still the enemy and the avenger! He might be a child, yet he was made to have dominion over the works of God's hands! Listen to his buoyant challenge in Psalm 18:

> For by thee I have run through a troop;
> And by my God have I leaped over a wall...
> It is God that girdeth me with strength...
> He maketh my feet like hind's feet...
> He teacheth my hands to war...thou hast subdued under me
> those that rose up against me (vv. 29, 32, 33, 34, 39).

Through faith David subdued kingdoms, stopped the mouths of lions, escaped the edge of the sword, waxed mighty in war, turned to flight armies of enemies.

PRUDENT IN SPEECH

The sagacity of David will appear as our story proceeds. David was as prudent to advise and scheme as he was swift to execute. He had an understanding of the times, of human hearts, of wise policy.

He knew just how and when to act. Honest with his friends, generous to his foes, constant in his friendships, calm in danger, patient in trouble, chivalrous and knightly, he had every element of a born leader of men. He was equally at home in the counsels of the state and the decisions of the battlefield. Whatever emergency threatened, David seems to know just how to meet it. And this was no doubt due to the repose of his spirit in God. The sad mistakes he made may be traced to his yielding to the sway of impulse and passion, to his forgetfulness of his habit of drawing near to God and inquiring of Him before taking any important step. The attitude of his soul is sweetly mirrored in one of his earliest psalms: "Because of his strength, will I wait upon thee.... Unto thee, O my strength, will I sing" (Psalm 59:9,17). When men live like that, they cannot fail to be prudent in speech and wise in counsel.

THE CHARM OF HIS PRESENCE

He was David the beloved. Wherever he moved, he cast the spell of his personal magnetism. Saul yielded to it and warmed. The servants of the royal household loved him. Michal, Saul's daughter, loved him. The soul of Jonathan was knit with David's soul. The women of Israel forgot their loyalty to Saul as they sounded the praises of the young hero who was so handsome. The wild, rough soldiers were willing to risk their lives to gratify David's wish for a drink from Bethlehem's well. So David passed through life, swaying the scepter of irresistible potency over men and women. The beautiful Abigail is glad to wash the feet of his servants. Achish says that he is an angel of the Lord. Ittai the Gittite clings to David in his exile. The people slink into the city because David is weeping over Absalom. When he speaks, the hearts of the men of Judah, conscious of treachery and slow to welcome him, are moved even as the heart of one man. Beloved of God and man, with a heart tremulous to the touch of love, the soil of David's soul was capable of bearing harvests to enrich the world. But his soul was also capable of the keenest suffering possible to man.

GOD WAS WITH HIM

David had no hesitation in describing himself as "thy servant," liable to hidden and presumptuous faults, from which he desired above all things to be delivered. He thought of God as his Rock,

Redeemer, Shepherd, and Host in the house of life, his Comforter in every darksome glen. In weariness David found green pastures; in thirst, still waters; in perplexity, righteous guidance; in danger, sure defense—through what the Lord was to his soul. God's Word, though David knew only a part of it, was perfect, right, and pure; and as David recited it to himself, under great nature's tent, it restored his soul, rejoiced his heart, enlightened his eyes, and seemed better than the honey that dripped from the rock. David set the Lord always before him; because He was at his right hand, he could not be moved, and therefore his heart was glad.

4

1 Samuel 17:11

A Dark Background

I flung away
Those keys that might have open set
The golden sluices of the day;
But clutch the keys of darkness yet.
I hear the reapers singing go
Into God's harvest; I that might
With them have chosen, here below
Grope shuddering at the gates of night.

J.R. Lowell

A great contrast, as we have said, is evidently intended by the historian between Saul and David. The portrait of Saul is drawn in Rembrandt colors to set forth the excelling beauty of God's designated king.

The king of Israel took his first step away from God when he allowed himself to be betrayed into undue haste and precipitation, performing the burnt offering at Michmash before Samuel came. Saul took further steps in the same direction in the outburst of indig-nation against Jonathan for violating his regulation about abstinence from food. But the final break took place when he disobeyed the distinct command of Jehovah through his prophet Samuel, sparing Agag and the best of the spoils of war. Then he rejected the word of the Lord, and God gave him up to his own evil heart. From that moment, his course was always downward toward the gathering gloom of Gilboa. From the disobedient heart, God withdraws His keeping power, and as it is no longer indwelt by the Spirit of the Most High, it becomes at once the prey and habitation of unclean spirits, reminding us of the awful words with which Isaiah describes the desolation of Edom (Isaiah 34:14–15).

Such was the state of Saul's heart. Since Saul was not willing to retain God in his knowledge, God gave him up to a reprobate mind to do those things that are not fitting.

I will highlight some points in Saul's dark eclipse that serve to illustrate prominent features in the young shepherd's character.

FORSAKEN BY THE SPIRIT OF GOD

Imagine the portrait of Saul amid the black mid-tent's silence, from which for days together not a sound came to the anxious watchers. It was the blackness of darkness reigning. Somewhere within, the figure of Saul is resting against the tent prop without movement, speech, or appetite for food. He shudders for a moment under the first spell of music, and then resumes his insensibility to all.

The departure of the Spirit of the Lord probably refers to that special equipment for the regal office that had once come mightily upon him. In Saul's case, it had rather to do with office than with any change of disposition and heart (1 Samuel 10:10; 11:6). By his willfulness and disobedience, Saul forfeited this royal prerogative. The light faded off his soul, and he became as other men.

Nothing in this world or the next can be compared for horror to the withdrawal of God from us. It involves the damnation of body and soul, because it is the one force by which evil is restrained and good fostered. Take the sun from the center of the solar system, and each planet, breaking from its leash, would pursue a headlong course, colliding with the rest and dashing into the abyss. So when God's presence is lost, every power in the soul rises in revolt. Ah, bitter wail, when a man realizes the true measure of the calamity that has befallen him and cries with Saul, "I am sore distressed; for...God is departed from me, and answereth me no more" (1 Samuel 28:15).

It is a very serious thing to ask if we are not tampering with the Spirit of the Lord. To do so will turn the most radiant dawn into the chill twilight of a wintry day when the blizzard fills the air with snow and ice. Beware lest you fret against the divine delays or disobey the divine command. We need to be aware of the things that belong to our peace lest they be forever hid from our view, and as the sun's last rim sinks beneath the waves, the storm clouds of jealousy, superstition, and frenzy bear down upon us in thick battalions.

How different with David! The Lord was with him. To the clear, bright eye of his faith, the living God was more real than the giant that stalked each morning before the hosts of Israel. Had He not delivered David from the paw of the lion and from the paw of the bear? And was He not as real amid the dignity of the court or the clash of the battlefield? The dew of the divine blessing rested upon that fair young head, and the light of the Shekinah shone from the inner shrine through those clear blue eyes. With him the Spirit of God was not simply an equipment of gift for service but was the resident presence of the divine in soul and heart.

TROUBLED BY AN EVIL SPIRIT FROM THE LORD

Evidently, the conception is of Jehovah surrounded by spirits—some good and some evil. He has only to speak, and one powerful to exercise a malign and deadly influence hastens to do His bidding. Micaiah spoke after the same manner in the dark hour of Ahab's infatuation (1 Kings 22:19–23). This method of speech is unfamiliar. We prefer to say that God allows evil spirits to fasten on souls that have refused Him, as vultures on the carcass from which life has fled. We go further and say that God always means to do the best by every creature that He has made, but that we have the power of extracting evil from His good, of transforming His sunshine and rain into hemlock and deadly nightshade and rank poison, of transmuting the roses that fall from His hand into the red-hot cinders that scorch and burn into the flesh.

Never doubt that God is good and that He sends good and gentle spirits to keep man from evil and to conduct him into the light of life. But when we turn against God, it seems as though He commences to be our enemy and to fight against us. The reality is that whereas we once went with the stream or the divine blessing, we are now wading against it with difficulty and peril. With the stubborn, God shows Himself stubborn; and with the perverse, His angels, conscience, gratitude, the memory of the past, convictions of duty that were intended to elevate and save, oppose their progress as mortal foes. They wrestle with us—or rather, we wrestle with them—in the dark night, in which we cannot distinguish friend from foe. So when Judas had finally chosen to betray our Lord, the very pleadings of Jesus hardened his heart and sealed his doom.

With David, on the other hand, the Spirit of God was constantly cooperating. David lived and walked in fellowship with the unseen. All the genial influences of heaven, as they fell upon his young spirit, elicited responses of love and faith like the strains of music that each passing breeze summons from the Eolian harp.

SAUL'S DISCORD

The fact that music was the corrective of the king's malady seems to indicate that being wrong with God, he was out of harmony with the universe. It is impossible to define music. In its grander and more lovely strains, it has escaped the defiling touch of sin and is, so to speak, the echo of eternity. Music is like the spray from the waves of light and glory that breaks upon our shores, the expression of the infinite order and rhythm of the spheres. Music, therefore, is the natural expression of the perfect life and peace of heaven. There the harpers play upon their harps; there redeemed and glorified spirits raise new songs; there holy beings express their perfect accord with the nature of God and the order of the universe in outbursts of harmonious sound. Perfected sense, which can be had only on the condition of unbroken union with God's will, purpose, and life, would detect all things uttering "Hallelujah!" and be compelled by the contagiousness of a holy sympathy to swell the anthem.

To all this Saul was a stranger. He was away from God, and there was consequently discord in his heart and life. Music falling on his ear recalled memories of his former better self and laid a brief spell upon the discordant elements of his soul, reducing them to a momentary order. But these were destined to be marred and spoiled as soon as the sweet sounds were withdrawn. Yes, it is always this way. If you are not at peace with God through Jesus Christ, you are at enmity through wicked works and inward temper. There can be, therefore, no sympathy between you and the universe around. Art, music, the engagements of daily business, the whirl of society, the exercises of religion may do what David's harp did for Saul, in producing a momentary stillness and sense of harmony with your environment, but it is only for a moment. When the spell is withdrawn, the old spirit of disorder asserts itself.

With David, on the other hand, the harp was the symbol of a soul at rest in God. All things were, therefore, his. All spoke to his soul of the harmonies subsisting in the unseen and eternal world. And it was because his own spirit was so perfectly harmonious with the nature of God and with the universe that he could cast the spell of calming and quieting influence over another. This may explain the influence of music in all ages of the world over the illnesses of the soul. Elisha called for a minstrel to calm his disquieted spirit. Pythagoras, as Seneca tells us, was in the habit of quieting the troubles of his mind with a harp. Philip V of Spain was recalled from the profoundest depression by the famous singer Farinelli.

The servants of Saul were therefore justified in urging him in one of his lucid moments to permit them to seek out a man who was a cunning player on the harp. And the power that David exercised over him is an illustration of a similar charm that we may individually exert upon the restless, storm-tossed spirits around us. Let us accept God's basis of the reconciliation. Let us stand beneath the cross of Christ, which is the center of reconciliation from the discords of sin, till we are in perfect accord with it. And let us go forth to induce men to come to that center also, to be reconciled to God, and to learn the mystery of that peace of which Jesus spoke on the eve of His death and the day of His resurrection.

Saul's Unbelief

If a man is wrong with God, faith is impossible, for it is the fruit of the soul. When, therefore, Goliath stalked through the valley of Elah and defied the armies of Israel, Saul was greatly afraid. Where was the prowess that engaged the early love and admiration of the people, that delivered Jabesh-gilead and vexed the foes of Israel wherever he turned himself? It had vanished as the beauty passes from the surface of the fruit that is rotten at the core. Under happier conditions, Saul would have become the champion of his people; now he cowered in his tent.

David, on the other hand, had no such fear. His soul was full of God. God was his light and salvation, whom should he fear? the strength of his life, of whom should he be afraid? David was hidden in the secret of God's pavilion and abode under the shadow of the Almighty. There was no unsteadiness in the hand that slung the stone, no tremor in the heart. David was strong in faith because his young heart was pure and good and right and in living fellowship with Jehovah.

5

1 Samuel 17

THE FAITH
OF GOD'S ELECT

Who the line
Shall draw, the limits of the power define
That even imperfect faith to man affords?

Wordsworth

*I*n the valley of Elah today, the traveler finds the remains of an immense terebinth. Perhaps this gave it its name: "the valley of the terebinth." Starting from the neighborhood of the ancient city of Hebron, the valley runs in a northwesterly direction toward the sea. It is about a mile across, and in the middle is a deep ravine, some twenty feet across with a depth of ten or twelve feet. Winter torrents have made this their track.

Having recovered from the chastisement inflicted on them by Saul and Jonathan at Michmash, the Philistines had marched up the valley of Elah, encamping on its western slope between Shochoh and Ephes-dammin (a name with an ominous meaning—"the boundary of blood"—probably because on more than one occasion it had been the scene of border forays). Saul pitched his camp on the other side of the valley. Behind them were the Judean hills, ridge on ridge, to the blue distance where Jerusalem lay as yet in the hands of the Jebusite. That valley was to witness an encounter that brought into fullest contrast the principles on which God's warriors are to contend—not only with flesh and blood but also against the principalities and powers of darkness. Three figures stand out sharply defined on that memorable day.

First, *the Philistine champion*. He was tall—nine feet six inches in height. He was heavily armed, for his armor fell as spoil to Israel, was eagerly examined, and minutely described. The Israelites even weighed it and found it to be five thousand shekels of brass, equivalent to two hundred pounds. He was protected by an immense shield that was carried by another in front of him so as to leave his arms and hands free. He wielded a ponderous spear, while a sword and javelin were attached to his side. He was skilled at the art of boasting, talked of the banquet he proposed to give to the fowls and beasts, and defied the armies of the living God.

Second, *Saul*. A fine young man and sizable. There was not among the children of Israel a more physical person than he; from his shoulders and upward he was taller than any of the people. He had also a good suit of armor, a helmet of brass, and a coat of mail. In earlier days, when he had blown the trumpet, its notes had run throughout the land, stirring all hearts with anticipations of certain victory. Even now the formula of his former faith and fervor came easily to his lips as he assured the young shepherd that the Lord would certainly be with him. But Saul dared not adventure himself in conflict with what he reckoned were utterly overwhelming odds. He was near to intimidating David with his materialism and unbelief: "Thou art not able to go against this Philistine to fight with him: for thou art but a youth, and he a man of war from his youth" (1 Samuel 17:33).

Third, *David*. He was but a youth, and ruddy, and withal of a fair countenance. No sword was in his hand. He carried a staff, probably his shepherd's crook. No armor had he on, save the breastplate of righteousness and the helmet of salvation. He had no weapon but a sling in his hand and five smooth stones that he had chosen out of the torrent bed and put in the shepherd's bag. But David was in possession of a mystic spiritual power that the mere spectator might have guessed but which he might have found it difficult to define. The living God was a reality to him. His countrymen were not simply, as Goliath insinuated, servants to Saul. They were the army of the living God. When David spoke of armies, using the plural, he may have been thinking of Jacob's vision of the host of angels at Mahanaim or of Joshua, when the angel of the covenant revealed himself as captain of the Lord's host that waited unseen under arms, prepared to cooperate with that which Israel's chieftain was about to lead across the Jordan. Cannot we imagine that to the lad's imagination the air was full of horses and chariots of fire, of those angel hosts who in later times he addressed as strong in might, hearkening to the voice of God and hastening to do His pleasure in all places of His dominion. At the least David had no doubt that the Lord would vindicate His glorious name and deliver into his hands this uncircumcised Philistine.

Heroic Faith Was Born In Secret And Nursed In Solitude

Day after day, David considered the heavens and earth, which appeared as one vast tent in which God dwelt. Nature was the material dwelling place of the eternal Spirit, who was as real to David's young heart as the works of His hands to his poet's eyes. God was as real to David as Jesse or his brothers or Saul or Goliath. David's soul had so rooted itself in this conception of God's presence that he bore it with him, undisturbed by the shout of the soldiers as they went forth to the battle and the searching questions addressed to him by Saul.

This is the unfailing secret. There is no shortcut to the life of faith, which is the all vital condition of a holy and victorious life. We must have periods of lonely meditation and fellowship with God. That our souls should have their mountains of fellowship, their valleys of quiet rest beneath the shadow of a great rock, their nights beneath the stars, when darkness has veiled the material and silenced the stir of human life and has opened the view of the infinite and eternal, is as indispensable as that our bodies should have food. Thus alone can the sense of God's presence become the fixed possession of the soul, enabling it to say repeatedly with the psalmist, "Thou art so near, O God."

HEROIC FAITH HAD BEEN
EXERCISED IN LONELY CONFLICT

With a beautiful modesty, David would probably have kept to himself the story of the lion and the bear, unless it had been extracted from him by a desire to magnify Jehovah. Possibly there had been many conflicts of a similar kind, so that his faith had become strengthened by use as the muscles of his wiry young body by exertion. In these ways he was being prepared for this supreme conflict.

What we are in solitude, we shall be in public. Do not for a moment suppose that the stimulus of a great occasion will endow you with a heroism of which you have shown no trace in secret hours. The crises will only reveal the true quality and temper of the soul. The flight of the disciples at the Master's arrest will make it almost needless for the historian to explain that the hour that should have been spent in watching was squandered in sleep. It is the universal testimony of holy men that lonely hours are full of temptation. It is in these that we must conquer if we would be victorious when the eyes of some great assembly are fastened upon us.

HEROIC FAITH STOOD
THE TEST OF DAILY LIFE

There are some who appear to think that the loftiest attainments of the spiritual life are incompatible with the grind of daily toil and the friction of the home. "Free us from these," they cry. "Give us nothing to do except to nurse our souls to noble deeds. Deliver us from the obligations of family ties, and we will fight for those poor souls who are engrossed with the cares and ties of the ordinary and commonplace."

It was not thus with David. When Jesse, eager to know how it fared with his three elder sons who had followed Saul to the battle, asked David to take them rations and a present to the captain of their division, there was an immediate and ready acquiescence in his father's proposal: "And David rose up early in the morning,... and took, and went, as Jesse had commanded him" (1 Samuel 17:20). And before he left his flock, David was careful to entrust it with a keeper. We must always watch not to neglect one duty for another. If we are summoned to the camp, we must first see to the tending of the flock. He who is faithful in the greater must first have been faithful in the least. It is in the home, at the office, and in the Sunday school that we are being trained for service at home and abroad. We must not forsake the training ground until we have learned all the lessons God has designed it to teach.

HEROIC FAITH BORE MEEKLY MISCONSTRUCTION AND REBUKE

Reaching the camp, David found the troops forming in battle array and ran to the front. He had already discovered his brothers and greeted them, when he was arrested by the braggart voice of Goliath from across the valley. There he saw, to his chagrin, the men of Israel turn to flee, stricken with sore fright. When he expressed surprise, David learned from bystanders that even Saul shared the general panic and had issued rewards for a champion. So David passed from one group to another, questioning, gathering further information of his first impressions, and finding everywhere the open-eyed wonder of his soul that any man's heart should fail because of Goliath.

Eliab had no patience with the words and bearing of his young brother. How dare David suggest that the behavior of the men of Israel was unworthy of themselves and religion! What did David mean by inquiring so minutely after the particulars of the royal reward? Was he thinking of winning it? It was absurd to talk like that! Of course, it could only be talk, but it was amazing to hear it suggested that David, too, was a soldier and qualified to fight. Evidently something needed to be said to knock David back into his rightful place and minimize the effect of his words and let the bystanders know who and what David was. "Why camest thou down hither? and with whom," Eliab said with a sneer, "hast thou left those few sheep in the wilderness?" (1 Samuel 17:28). Ah, what venom lay in those few words! David, however, ruled his spirit and answered softly. "Sure," said he, "my father's wish to learn of your welfare was cause enough to bring me here." It was there that the victory over Goliath was really won. To have lost his temper in this unprovoked assault would have broken the alliance of his soul with God and drawn a veil over David's sense of His presence. But to meet evil with good and maintain an unbroken composure not only showed the burnished beauty of his spirit's armor but also cemented his alliance with the Lamb of God.

To bear with unfailing meekness the spiteful attacks of malice and envy, to not be overcome by evil but to overcome evil with good, to suffer wrong, to possess one's soul in patience, to keep the mouth with a bridle when the wicked is before us, to pass unruffled and composed through a tornado of unkindness and misrepresentation—this is possible only to those in whose breasts the dovelike Spirit has found an abiding place and whose hearts are guarded by the peace of God. These are they who bear themselves as heroes in the fight. A marvelous exhibition was given that day in the valley of Elah that those who are gentlest under provocation are strongest in the fight and that meekness is really an attribute of might.

Heroic Faith Withstood the Reasonings Of The Flesh

Saul was very eager for David to use his armor, though he dared not wear it himself. He was taken with the boy's sincerity of spirit but advised him to adopt the means. "Don't be rash; don't expect a miracle. By all means trust God, and go, but be wise. We should adopt ordinary precautions."

It was a critical hour. Had David turned aside to act on these suggestions, he would certainly have forfeited the divine alliance that was conditioned by his guileless faith. There is no sin in using means, but they must come second, not first. The means must be such as God suggests. It is a sore temptation to adopt them as indicated by the flesh and hope that God will bless them instead of waiting before Him to know what He would have done and how. How often has the advice of worldly prudence dampened the eager aspiration of the spirit and hindered the doing of a great deed?

But an unseen hand withdrew David from the meshes of temptation. He had already yielded so far to Saul's advice as to have put on the armor and taken up the sword. Then David turned to Saul and said, "I cannot go with these," and he put them off. It was not now Saul's armor *and* the Lord, but the Lord alone, and David was able without hesitation to accost the giant with the words: "The Lord saveth not with sword and spear" (1 Samuel 17:47).

David's faith had been put to the severest tests and was approved. Being more precious than silver or gold, it had been exposed to the most searching ordeal, but the furnace of trial had shown it to be of heavenly temper. Now let Goliath do his worst; he shall know that there is a God in Israel.

6

1 Samuel 17:45

IN THE NAME OF
THE LORD OF HOSTS

Oh, I have seen the day,
When with a single word,
God helping me to say,
"My trust is in the Lord"!
My soul hath quenched a thousand foes,
fearless of all that could oppose.

Cowper

While the two armies waited expectantly on either side of the ravine, every eye was suddenly attracted by the slight young figure who, with staff in hand, emerged from the ranks of Israel and descended the slope. For a little while, David was hidden from view as he bent intent over the pebbles that lined the bottom, from which he selected five smooth stones and placed them in his shepherd's bag. Then, to the amazement of the Philistines, and especially of their huge champion, David sprang up on the further bank and rapidly moved toward Goliath.

Goliath had apparently been sitting, and when he realized that the youth was daring to accept his challenge, he arose and came, drawing near to meet David. He cursed David as he did so, threatening him that his blood should encrimson the mountain grass while his unburied body feasted the wild things of earth and air. Then said David to the Philistine: "Thou comest to me with a sword, and with a spear, and with a shield: but I come to thee in the name of the LORD of hosts, the God of the armies of Israel, whom thou hast defied" (1 Samuel 17:45).

THE DECLARATION OF VICTORY

"The name of the LORD of Hosts." Throughout the Scriptures, a name is not simply a label. It is a revelation of character. It catches up and enshrines some moral or physical peculiarity in which its owner differs from other men or which constitutes his special gift and force. The names that Adam gave the animals that were brought to him were founded on characteristics that struck his notice. And the names that Jesus Christ gave to the apostles either expressed qualities that lay deep within them or unfolded some great purpose for which they were being fitted.

Thus the name of God, as used so frequently by the heroes and saints of sacred history, stands for those divine attributes and qualities that combine to make Him what He is. In the history of the early Church, *the Name* was a kind of summary of all that Jesus had revealed of the nature and the heart of God. "For his name's sake they went forth, taking nothing of the Gentiles" (3 John 7). There was no need to specify whose Name it was—there was no other Name that could be compared or mentioned on the same page. Stars die out and become invisible when the sun appears. That Name is above every name, and to it every knee shall bow and every tongue confess because it embodies under one all-sufficient designation everything that any single soul, or the whole race, can require or imagine or attain in the conceiving of God.

The special quality that David extracted from the bundle of qualities represented by the divine Name of God is indicated in the words, *the Lord of hosts*. That does not mean only that God was Captain of the embattled hosts of Israel; that idea was expressed in the words that followed: "The God of the armies of Israel." But there was probably something of this sort in David's thought. David conceived of angels and worlds, of the armies of heaven and the elements of matter, of winds and waves, of life and death, as a vast ordered army, obedient to the commands of their Captain, Jehovah of Hosts. In fact, David's idea was identical to the heathen centurion of the gospels, who said he was a man under authority, having servants to whom he said, Come, or Go, or Do this or that.

To come in the Name of the Lord of Hosts did not simply mean that David understood Jehovah to be all this, but it also implied his own identification by faith with all that was comprehended in this sacred Name. An Englishman in a foreign land occupies a very different position and speaks in a very different tone according to whether he assumes a private capacity as an ordinary traveler or acts as a representative and ambassador of his country. In the former case, he speaks in his own name and receives what respect and obedience it can obtain. In the latter, he is conscious of being identified with all that is associated with the term *Great Britain*. For a man to speak in the name of England means that England speaks through his lips, that the might of England is ready to enforce his demands, and that every sort of power that England wields is pledged to avenge any affront or indignity to which he may be exposed.

Thus, when Jesus bids us ask what we will in His Name, He does not mean that we should simply use that name as an incantation or formula, but He means that we should be so one with Him in His interests, purposes, and aims that it should be as though He were Himself approaching the Father with the petitions we bear.

There is much for us to learn concerning this close identification with God before we shall be able to say with David, "I come to thee in the name of the LORD of hosts." It is possible only to those who carefully fulfill certain conditions that were familiar enough to this divinely taught youth. It is well worth our while to withdraw from the activities of our life, to lay aside everything that might hinder the closeness of our union with the divine nature and interest, and to become so absolutely identified with God that His Name might be our strong tower, our refuge, our battle cry, our secret of victory. Oh, to be able to approach every high-handed wrongdoer, each confederacy of evil, each assault of the powers of darkness, each tribe of savages, each drink-sodden district, each congregation of the unsaved and impenitent, with the words, "I come in the name of the LORD of hosts"!

The Conditions We Are Warranted For Using The Name

When we are pure in our motives. There was no doubt as to the motive that prompted David to this conflict. It is true that he had spoken to the men of Israel, saying, "What shall be done to the man that killeth the Philistine?" but no one supposed that he acted as he did because of the royal reward. David's one ambition was to take away the reproach from Israel and to let all the earth know that there was a God in Israel.

We must be wary here. It is so easy to confuse issues and to suppose that we are contending for the glory of God when we are really combatting for our church, our cause, our prejudices, or our opinions. It has always been a temptation to sincere men to veil from their own eyes the selfishness of their motives and aims by insisting, with vehement declarations, that they are actuated by pure zeal for the cause of God.

To fall into this sin, though unconsciously, is to forfeit the right to use His sacred Name. We may still plead with it and invoke it, but in vain. The very demons we seek to bind as with a spell will deride us, leaping out and chasing us before them. How constantly we need to expose our hearts to the inspiration of the Holy Spirit, that He may wholly cleanse them and fill them with an all-consuming devotion to the glory of God. May the words be true of us as of our Lord: "The zeal of thine house hath eaten me up" (John 2:17).

When we are willing to allow God to occupy His rightful place. David said repeatedly that the whole matter was God's. David might gather up the spoils of the battle, but the overthrow of Goliath and the Philistine host was not in his province at all. "The battle is the LORD's,... This day will the LORD deliver thee into mine hand;... He will give you into our hands" (1 Samuel 17:46-47).

David's attitude has been that of every man who has wrought great exploits in the behalf of righteousness. Moses said, "The LORD God...appeared unto me,...and...[he] will bring you up out of the affliction of Egypt" (Exodus 3:16-17). Samuel said, "Prepare your hearts unto the LORD,...and he will deliver you out of the hand of the Philistines" (1 Samuel 7:3). Paul said, "I will not dare to speak of any of those things which Christ hath not wrought by me" (Romans 15:18). We must recognize Jesus Christ as the essential warrior, worker, organizer, and administrator of His Church through the Holy Spirit. Whatever is rightly done He must do. We are called not to work for Him but to let Him work through us. Of Him and through Him and to Him are all things. The battle is not ours, but

His. His skill must direct us; His might must empower us; His up-lifted hands bring us victory.

When we dare take no counsel with the flesh. It must have been hard for a youth to oppose his opinion to Saul's, especially when the king was so caring for his welfare. "Spare yourself, my son," Saul seemed to say. "Be wise, take ordinary precautions, do not throw your young life away." It was a dangerous moment. To meet scorn, hatred, and wrongdoing with uncompromising defiance and resistance is so much easier than to refuse assistance or advice that is meant kindly. It was excellent that David withstood the siren song and remained unaffected by the coaxing of royal favor. He could not have served two masters so utterly antagonistic. To have yielded to Saul would have put him beyond the fire ring of the divine environment.

How perpetually does Satan breathe into our ears the soft words that Peter whispered to his Master when he began to speak about the cross: "Spare thyself: that shall not come unto thee." There is so much talk about the legitimacy of means that no room is left for the Almighty to act. Means are good in their rightful place, but that place is far from first. Both their nature and time have to be fixed by Him who refuses helmets of brass and coats of armor, that no flesh should glory in His presence but he who uses the rustic sling, the smooth stone from the brook, and the sword of Goliath.

The Bearing Of
Those Who Use The Name

They are willing to stand alone. The lad asked no companions in the fight. There was no running to and fro to secure a second person. David was perfectly prepared to bear the whole brunt of the fray without sympathy or help. He was that sure that the Lord of Hosts was with him and that the God of Jacob was his refuge.

They are deliberate. David was free from the nervousness and fear that so often prevent us from playing our part in some great scene. Our heart will throb so quickly, our movements become so fitful and unsteady. Calmly and quietly David went down the slope and selected the pebbles that best suited his purpose. In this quiet-ness and confidence he found his strength. His mind was kept in perfect peace because it was stayed on God. He did not go by haste or flight, because the Lord went before him and the Holy One of Israel was his reward.

They are fearless. When the moment came for the conflict, David did not hesitate but ran toward the Philistine army to meet their champion. There was no fear of the result in that young heart, no tremor in the voice that answered the rough taunt, no falter in the arm that wielded the sling, no lack of precision in the aim that drove the stone to the one part of the Philistine's body that was unprotected and vulnerable.

They are more than conquerors. The stone sank into the giant's forehead, and in another moment he fell stunned to the earth. There was no time to lose. Before Goliath could recover himself, or his startled comrades overcome their stupefied amazement, his head had been hewn from his body by one thrust of his own sword. And when the Philistines saw that their champion was dead, they fled. The spoils of victory lay with the victor. David took the head of the Philistine as a trophy and put his armor in his tent.

Let us live alone with God. The weakest man who knows God is strong to do exploits. All the power of God awaits the disposal of our faith. As a child by touching a lever may set in motion a mighty ocean liner, making it glide like a swan into her native element, so a child who has learned to count on God may bring the whole forces of deity to bear on men and things on the world's battlefield. This is the victory that overcomes the world, the flesh, and the devil—even our faith.

7

1 Samuel 18:1

JONATHAN

Souls that carry on a blest exchange
Of joys they meet within their heavenly range,
And, with a fearless confidence, make known
The sorrows sympathy esteems its own—
Daily derive increasing light and force
From such communion in their pleasant course;
Feel less the journey's roughness and its length,
Meet their opposers with united strength;
And one in heart, in interest, and design,
Gird up each other to the race divine.

Cowper

In heaven's vault there are what are known as binary stars, two suns with their attendant train of worlds, revolving around each other but blending their rays so that they reach the watcher's eye as one clear beam of light. So do twin souls find the center of their orbit in each other. And there is nothing in the annals of human affection nobler than the bond of such a love between two pure, high-minded, and noble men, whose love passes that of women. Such love was celebrated in ancient classic story and has made the names of Damon and Pythias proverbial. It has also enriched the literature of modern days in the love of a Hallam and a Tennyson. But nowhere is it more fragrant than on the pages that contain the memorials of the love of Jonathan and David.

David was in all probability profoundly influenced by the character of Jonathan, who must have been considerably older than he. It seems to have been a nearly instant love. "When [David] had made an end of speaking unto Saul,...the soul of Jonathan was knit with the soul of David, and Jonathan loved him as his own soul" (1 Samuel 18:1). He did not, however, openly acknowledge it on the spot, but that night, as the young shepherd was sitting amidst a group of soldiers, recounting with them the events of the memorable day, a royal messenger may have summoned him to Jonathan's pavilion. Upon entering, David was amazed to be greeted with the warm embrace of a brotherly affection that was never to wane. He had lost Eliab in the morning, but at nightfall he had won a friend who would stick closer than a brother. The young David must have shrunk back as unworthy—looking down ruefully at his poor apparel as unbefitting a royal alliance. But all such considerations were swept sway before the impetuous rush of Jonathan's affection, as he stripped himself of robe and apparel, of sword and bow and girdle, and gave them all to David. "Then Jonathan and David made a covenant, because he loved him as his own soul" (1 Samuel 18:3).

THE QUALITIES OF THIS FRIEND

Consider the type of friend whom Jehovah chose for the molding of the character of His beloved David, and then be prepared to surrender to His care the choice of your most intimate associates. He knows what your temperament needs and where to find the companion who shall strengthen you when weak and develop latent unknown qualities.

He was every inch a man. In true friendship, there must be a similarity of tastes and interests. The prime condition of two men walking together is that they should be agreed, and the bond of a common manliness knit these twin souls from the first. Jonathan was every inch a man and was as dexterous with the bow as his friend with his sling. Able to flash with indignation, strong to bear without quailing the brunt of his father's wrath, fearless to espouse the cause of his friends at whatever cost, Jonathan was capable of inspiring a single armor bearer with his own ardent spirit of attacking an army, of turning the tide of invasion, and of securing the admiration and affection of the entire people who, standing between him and his father, refused to let him die. When Jonathan fell on Gilboa, it was no exaggeration that led David to lament: "The beauty of Israel is slain upon thy high places: how are the mighty fallen!" (2 Samuel 1:19).

He was very sensitive and tender. It is fashionable in some quarters to emphasize the qualities supposed to be specially characteristic of men—those of strength, courage, endurance—to the undervaluing of the tenderer graces more often associated with women. But in every true man there must be a touch of woman, as there was in the ideal Man, the Lord Jesus. In Him there is neither male nor female, because there is the symmetrical blending of both. In us, too, there should be strength and sweetness, courage and sympathy; the oak and the vine, the rock and the moss that covers it with its soft green mantle.

Jonathan had a marvelous power of affection. He loved David as himself. He was prepared to gladly surrender his succession to his father's throne if only he might be next to his friend. His was the love that expresses itself in tender embraces and tears that must have response from the object of its choice:

> I am distressed for thee, my brother Jonathan:
> very pleasant hast thou been unto me:
> thy love to me was wonderful,
> passing the love of women (2 Samuel 1:26).

We judge a man by his friends and the admiration he excites in them. Any man whom David loved must have been possessed of many of those traits so conspicuous in David himself. Much is said of the union of opposites, and it is well when one is rich where the other is poor. But the deepest love must be between those whose natures are close akin. As we, therefore, review the love that united these two now forever joined in the indissoluble bonds of eternity, we must attribute to Jonathan the poetic sensitiveness, the tender emotion, the heroism of that courage, the capacity for those uprisings of the soul to all that was pure and lovely and noble, which were so conspicuous in David.

He was a true believer. When we are first introduced to Jonathan, he is accompanied by his armor bearer as he climbs singlehanded to attack the Philistine garrison, which was strongly entrenched behind rocky crags. He speaks as one familiar with the ways of God, to whom there is no restraint "to save by many or by few." And when the appointed sign is given, it is accepted as a presage of the victory that the Lord is about to give (1 Samuel 14).

As Jonathan stands beside his father on the hillside and sees the stripling descend to slay Goliath, winning a great victory for Israel, he discerns the hand of the Lord working a great victory for Israel, and his soul lifts itself in holy thought and thanksgiving (1 Samuel 19:5).

When the two friends are about to be torn from each other, with little hope of renewing their blessed relationship, Jonathan finds solace in the fact of the divine appointment and the Lord being between them. Between them, not in the sense of division, but of connection, as the ocean unites us with distant lands. However far we are parted from those we love, we are intimately near in God, whose presence infills and enwraps up—thus streams mingle in the ocean to which they pour tributary tides.

And when, in the last meeting the friends had, "Jonathan... went to David into the wood and strengthened his hand in God" (1 Samuel 23:16). All that those words imply it is not easy to write. Our hearts interpret the words and imagine the stream of holy encouragement that poured from that noble spirit into the heart of his friend. He must be strong who would strengthen another. He must have God and be in God who would give the consolations of God to his brother. And we can easily understand how the anguish of Jonathan's soul, torn between filial devotion to his father and his love for his friend, must have driven him back on those resources of the divine nature that are the only solace of men whose lives have been cast in the same fiery crucible.

THE CONFLICT OF JONATHAN'S LIFE

Jonathan was devoted to his father. He was always found associated with that strange dark character, melancholy to madness, the prey of evil spirits, and yet so keenly susceptible to music and so quick to respond to the appeal of chivalry, patriotism, and generous feeling. They resembled some mountain lake, alternately mirroring mountains and skies and swept by dark storms. Father and son were together in life, as they were "undivided in death."

When his father first ascended the throne of Israel, the Lord was with him, and Jonathan knew it (1 Samuel 20:13). It must have been an exceeding delight to him to feel that the claims of the father were identical with the claims of God, and the heart of the young man must have leaped up in a blended loyalty to both. But the fair prospect was soon overcast. The Lord departed from Saul, and immediately Saul's power to hold the kingdom waned. The Philistines invaded his land, his weapons of defense failed him, his people followed him trembling, and Samuel told him that his kingdom could not continue. Then followed that dark day when Saul intruded on the priestly office in offering sacrifice. The ominous sentence was spoken, "The LORD hath sought him a man after his own heart, and the LORD hath commanded him to be captain over his people" (1 Samuel 13:14).

From that moment, Saul's course was always downward. But Jonathan clung to his father as if he hoped that by his own allegiance to God he might reverse the effects of his father's failure and still hold the kingdom for their race.

At first this was not so difficult. There was no one to divide his heart with his father. It was not, therefore, a hardship for him to imperil his life in unequal conflict with the Philistines. And his heart must have been fired with the gladdest anticipations as, through the woods where honey dropped, he pursued the Philistines with all Israel at his heel, smiting them from Michmash to Aijalon. His hopes, however, were destined to disappointment, for instead of the revival that he had pictured to himself, he saw his father drifting further down the strong tide that bore him out from God. Saul's failure in the matter of the destruction of the Amalekites, the dark spirit that possessed and terrified him, the alienation of Samuel—these things acted as a moral paralysis on that brave and eager heart. What could Jonathan do to reverse the decisions of that fated soul, to stem the torrent, to turn the enemy from the gate? Surely it was this hopelessness of being able to alter any of these things that made Jonathan unable to meet Goliath. Many a time as he heard the terrible roar of the giant's challenge, he must have felt the uprisings of a noble impulse to meet him, slay him, or die. But there came over his soul the blight of despair. What could he do, when the destiny of the land he loved seemed already settled?

When Jonathan woke up to find how truly he loved David, a

new difficulty entered his life. Not outwardly, because, though Saul eyed David with jealousy, there was no open contention. David went in and out of the palace, was in a position of trust, and was constantly at hand for the friendship that each yearned. But when the flames of hostility, long smoldering in Saul's heart, broke forth, the true anguish of his life began. On the one hand, Jonathan's duty as son and subject held him to his father, though he knew his father was doomed and that union with David meant disaster to himself; on the other hand, all his heart cried out for David.

His love for David made him eager to promote reconciliation between his father and his friend. It was only when repeated failure had proved the fruitlessness of his dream that he abandoned it. And then the thought must have suggested itself to him: Why not escape the sinking ship while there is time? Why not join your fortunes with his whom God has chosen? The new fair kingdom of the future is growing up around him—identify yourself with it, though it be against your father.

The temptation was reasonable and masterful, but it fell blunt and ineffectual at Jonathan's feet. Stronger than the ties of human love were those of duty, sonship, loyalty to God's anointed king. In some supreme moment, Jonathan turned his back on the appeal of his heart and elected to stand beside his father. From that choice he never flinched. When David departed, Jonathan went back to the city. His father might sneer at his league with the son of Jesse, but he held his peace. And even when Saul started for his last battle with the Philistines, Jonathan fought beside him, though he knew that David was somehow involved in alliance with them.

It was one of the grandest exhibitions of the triumph of principle over passion, of duty over desire, that the annals of history record. Jonathan died as a hero, not only because of his prowess in battle over his country's foes but also because of his victory over the strongest passion of the human heart—the love of a strong man, in which were blended the strands of a common faith, a common enthusiasm for all that was good and right.

Conflicts like these await us all: when the appointment of God says one thing and the choice of the heart says another, when the wind sets in from one direction and the tide crashes in from the opposite direction. Whenever this befalls you, may God's grace enable you to follow as straight a course, as true to the loftiest dictates of conscience, as Jonathan, the son of Saul!

8

Psalm 59:9, 17

OUTSIDE THE HOUSE, AND IN

Unholy phantoms from the deep arise,
And gather through the gloom before mine eyes;
But all shall vanish at the dawning ray—
When the day breaks the shadows flee away.

He maketh all things good unto his own,
For them in every darkness light is strewn;
He will make good the gloom of this day—
Till that day break and shadows flee away.

S.J. Stone

*I*n the Hebrew, the difference between the words *wait* and *sing* as they appear in these passages is very slight. The words are spelled alike in the Hebrew, with the exception of a single letter. The parallelism between these two verses is therefore very marked:

> Because of his strength will I *wait* upon thee: for God is my defence (Psalm 59:9).
> Unto thee, O my strength, will I *sing:* for God is my defence (Psalm 59:17).

The inscription indicates the occasion on which this psalm—one of the oldest—was written: "A Psalm of David: when Saul sent,

51

and they watched the house to kill him." The allusions of the psalm substantiate this title, especially that of the sixth and fourteenth verses, in which the psalmist compares the troop of soldiers who encamped around his house, belching out their curses and threats, to the vicious curs of an Eastern city that prowl the streets by day and night, clearing them of their entrails and refuse and filling the night with their uproar:

> They return at evening: they make a noise like a dog,
> and go round about the city.
> Behold, they belch out with their mouth (vv. 6-7).

Meanwhile, David is in his house, waiting upon God and singing aloud of His mercy in the morning.

What Led Up To
This Assault On David's House

As the victorious army returned home from the valley of Elah, the whole land went forth in greeting. The reapers stopped their labors in the field, and the vineyards were depleted of the women who plucked the grapes and of the men who trod them in the presses. From village to town the contagious enthusiasm spread. The women came forth out of all the cities of Israel, with song and dance, with timbrels and tabrets, to meet King Saul. To the song of victory there came a refrain that was strikingly discordant to the soul of the king: "Saul hath slain his thousands, and David his ten thousands" (1 Samuel 18:7).

In that hour, the first jealous thought awoke in Saul's heart. It was like a pitted speck becoming visible in the good fruit of his character, which was destined to rot and ruin all. How happy he would have been had he trodden the hell spark beneath his feet or extinguished it in seas of prayer. But he nursed it until, to change the simile, the trickling stream undermined the seawall and became a raging turbid flood. "Saul was very wroth, and the saying displeased him;...And Saul eyed David from that day and forward" (1 Samuel 18:8-9).

But Saul was more than jealous. He deliberately set himself to thwart God's purpose. Samuel had distinctly told him that the Lord had rent the kingdom of Israel from him and given it to a neighbor of his who was better than he. And without doubt, as he saw the young man return with Goliath's head in his hand and as he heard the song of the Israelite women, the dread certainty suggested itself to him that this was the divinely designated king. "What though he be," said Saul to himself, as Herod in later days, "I am king and will see to it that this prediction at least shall not come true. A dead man cannot reign, and there are many ways short of direct murder by which a man's life can be taken. But this is what it must come to." Saul supposed that if only he could take David's life, God's purpose would miscarry and Samuel's predictions be falsified. He is not the last man who has descended into the arena to match himself with God and been crushed in the attempt. No student of history is likely to forget the cry of Julian the Apostate that mirrors the experience of thousands more: "Thou hast conquered, O Galilean!"

Saul's murderous passion sought to fulfill itself in many ways. On the following day, as David played to soothe Saul with his harp, Saul twice hurled his javelin at the minstrel in the hope that if it pinned him to the wall the act might be imputed to insanity. But on each occasion, the weapon sped harmlessly past, to quiver in the wall behind instead of in that young heart.

Next, Saul gave David an important military commission, making him captain over a thousand in the vain hope that this sudden elevation into the slippery place of worldly prominence and power might turn David's head dizzy and lead him to some traitorous deed for which death would be the obvious penalty. But David behaved himself wisely in all his ways, avoiding every pitfall, eluding every snare. So King Saul, who watched closely for David's falling, became more than ever convinced that David was God's ward and stood in awe of him.

Then Saul offered the young soldier the hand of his eldest daughter in marriage but treacherously withdrew the offer as the time of the wedding approached. Saul's intention was to arouse David's ardent spirit to retaliate and so to become liable to the charge of treason. But all his efforts failed to arouse even a transient impulse for revenge.

Again, by the lure of his second daughter Michal, as the prize to be won by the evidence of one hundred Philistines having been slain, Saul sought to involve his rivals in frays out of which only a miracle could bring him unhurt. But David returned unscathed with double the number required, and the love of the people grew.

Thwarted thus far, the godforsaken monarch, driven by the awful fury of his jealousy, spoke to Jonathan and to all his servants that they should rid him of David's tormenting presence. But this plot failed, for Jonathan delighted much in David, while all Israel and Judah loved him, for he went out and came in before them. Jonathan indeed stood in the breach to turn away his father's anger and elicited from him the promise that his friend should not be put to death. But his pleadings and reasonings had only a temporary effect, for shortly after, as the young minstrel endeavored to charm away Saul's spirit of melancholy, the javelin again quivered past him from the royal hand and would have transfixed him to the wall except for his lithe agility. It was the evening, and David fled to his young wife and home. And Saul, intent on murder, "sent messengers unto David's house, to watch him, and to slay him in the morning" (1 Samuel 19:11).

Michal's quick wit saved her husband's life. She let David down through the window, and David escaped. An image, covered with a quilt and placed in the bed, led Saul's emissaries to suppose that David was sick. There was no real occasion, however, for Michal to resort to trickery in securing David's safety from her father's murderous rage, for when, shortly after, the king proposed to snatch his prey from the midst of the company of prophets and from the very presence of Samuel, three sets of messengers were rendered powerless by the divine inspiration, and an arrest was put upon Saul himself, who was prostrated before the mighty impression of God's Spirit and lay helpless on the earth (1 Samuel 19:24).

That must have been a marvelous experience for David. To the eye of common sense, there was absolutely nothing to prevent the king's messengers or the king himself from taking him. But by faith David knew that he was being kept within the curtains of an impalpable pavilion and that he was hidden beneath an invisible wing. As the raying forth of Christ's majesty flung His captors to the ground, so did the presence of God surround and protect both Samuel and David. And thus our God will still do for each of His persecuted ones.

DAVID'S COMPOSURE AMID THE ASSAULTS OF HIS FOES

This hunted man is a lesson for men and angels. Saul is his inveterate foe, laying traps and snares for David on all sides. Sometimes the sun shines on David's golden locks, but more often the skies are thick with cloud and storm. One day the women of Israel welcome David, and then David is torn from his wife and driven forth from his home to go wherever he may. Yet all the while, David's heart is tranquil and reposed. David actually breaks forth into praise, as the closing verses of many of his psalms prove. What was the secret of David's serenity?

The secret lay, first, in the conviction of who God was. God was David's *strength*—that was God within him. God was his *defense*—that was God without and around him. David was God-possessed and God-encompassed. God dwelt in him, and he in God. There was no demand for which God was not sufficient, no peril that God could not keep at bay. What a blessed conception is here! You are too weak for some great task that has been entrusted to your care. In your judgment it would task the energies of the best and wisest you know, but it has been placed in your hands. "O Lord," you cry, "how shall I save Israel? Behold, my family is the poorest in Manasseh, and I am the least in my father's house." Then the Spirit of God reveals God as strength, that He may be so received into the heart as to become the principle of a new and heaven-born energy that shall rise superior to every difficulty and overcome the mightiest waves that would beat the swimmer back. Listen to the laughter of the apostle's soul as he surveys Herculean tasks on the one hand and enormous opposing obstacles on the other, saying with unhesitating assurance, "I can do all things through Christ which strengtheneth me" (Philippians 4:13). O weakest of the weak, remember Jesus Christ and take Him to be the strength of your life. Be strong in the grace that is in Christ Jesus.

Or turn to the other image. See those fugitive soldiers, hotly pursued by their enemies as clouds before the Biscay gale. On yonder cliff is perched a fortress, with mighty walls and towers of protection, if only they can be reached. Breathlessly, they scale the ascent, rush across the drawbridge, let down the portcullis, and fling themselves on the sward, knowing they are safe. God is all that to the soul that has learned to put Him between itself and everything. We do not even have to flee to God, for that implies that we have been allured away from Him. But we are to abide in Him, to stand fast in the liberty wherewith He has made us free, and to reckon that whatever Satan may say and however he may rage, we are absolutely secure so long as we abide in God.

After we realize these things, we need to add the other image with which Psalm 59 closes: that God is the fount of mercy. When we dare to believe that there is mercy in Saul's hate, mercy in the difficulties of our life, mercy in the clouds that veil our sky and the sharp stones that line our path, mercy in the bitterest experiences, then we can sing and say with David:

> But I will sing of thy power;
> yea, I will sing aloud of thy mercy in the morning:
> for thou hast been my defence and refuge in the day of my
> trouble (v. 16).

The secret of David's security lay, next, in his attitude toward God: "Because of his strength, will I *wait* on thee." The word *wait* is used in the Hebrew of the shepherd watching his flock, of the watchman on the tower, of the sentry passing to and fro upon his beat. Is this our habitual attitude? Too many believers direct their prayer but fail to look up the ladder for the descending angels, laden with the heavenly answer. Many a ship passes in the night, touching at our wharf with the precious freight that we have been praying for, but we are not there to receive it. Many a relieving force comes up the pass with glittering spears and flashing helmets, but our gates are closed. Many a dove comes to our window from the desolate waters, but we are too immersed in other things to notice its light tap. We pray, but we do not wait. We ask, but we do not expect to receive. We knock, but we are gone before the door is opened.

This lesson is for us to learn—to count upon God, to tarry for the vision, to wait till Samuel comes, to believe that He who taught us to trust cannot deceive our trust, to be sure that none of them who wait on Him can be ashamed, to appropriate by faith, and to know that we have the petitions we desire, nay, to do more, to take them and count them ours, though we have no responsive emotion, no sense of possession. This is waiting upon God. This will keep us calm and still, though dreaded evils frown around our homestead. This will change our waiting into song.

9

1 Samuel 20:21–37

THE MESSAGE
OF THE ARROWS

Toils and foes assailing, friends quailing, hearts failing
Shall threat in vain:
If He be providing, presiding, and guiding
To Him again.

J.M. Neal

*J*onathan had considerable influence with his father. Saul did nothing, either great or small, that he did not "uncover to his ear." For his love's sake as well as for his father's, Jonathan was extremely eager to effect a reconciliation between him to whom he owed the allegiance of son and subject and this fair shepherd-minstrel-warrior, who had so recently cast a sunny gleam upon his life. In all probability, Jonathan was much older than David, but in his pure and noble breast, the fountain of love rose unquenched by years. On more than one occasion he had communed with his father concerning his friend, so far impressing Saul as to make him swear that David should not be put to death. Thus, when David returned in hot haste from Naioth, leaving Saul under the spell of prophecy, and asked him what he had done to arouse such deep hate, asserting that there was but a step between him and death, Jonathan did not hesitate to assure him of his willingness to do whatever his soul desired.

It was the eve of the feast of the new moon when Saul invited the chief men of his kingdom to a banquet, and Jonathan and David agreed that this was an opportune moment for testing the real sentiments of Saul. David suggested that he should be absent from the royal banquet, visiting his father's home at Bethlehem instead. It would be quite easy for him to do this and yet be back by the third day. In the meantime, Jonathan was to carefully watch his father's behavior and mark his tone, noting whether it was rough or kind.

The general outline of this scheme was arranged within the palace, but there were confidences to be exchanged so intimate, words to be said so tender, a covenant to be entered into so moving, a means of communication to be arranged so secret, that it seemed wiser to continue the conversation in some secluded spot, where only the creatures of the woods that can tell no tales could behold the flowing tears and hear the outbreak of those manly sobs that could not be choked down. There was indeed one other witness, for Jonathan was a man of faith. It was his habit to live in the presence of the God of Israel, and to Him he made his appeal as he bared his heart to his friend, entreating him to deal truly with him and pleading that in that certain future, when God had cut off David's enemies from the earth, he would not forget the claims of friendship and cut off his kindness from his house.

Surely the fateful field of Gilboa was already casting a premonitory shadow over Jonathan's heart, and Jonathan felt the time would come when David would exercise supreme power and might be tempted to stamp out the possibility of rivalry on the part of Jonathan's heirs by exterminating the royal house. In his anxiety, Jonathan made David swear again and afterward proposed the ingenious and significant plan in which his art and directions to the little lad would express by a swift telegraphy the secret that would either lift David to peace and safety or thrust him into the depths of despair.

It is impossible to read the story without thinking of the boys who carry the envelopes, so little conscious of what the messages may mean to those in whose hands they place them, filling them with ecstasy or bitter anguish. The arrows are flying still. The little lads are fulfilling their unconscious ministries with respect to them. Often they fall short of the mark, then again they fly beyond it. How often they are beyond! O strong arm, why shoot them with so much energy? O wind, why carry them so lightly? Hearts are breaking as the bowstring twangs. Lives take their color of light or shadow ever after, just because of a few yards less or more!

THE ARROWS TAUGHT THAT A STRONG AND NOBLE FRIEND WAS STANDING IN THE BREACH

Jonathan was a jewel of the highest order, unequalled in his use of arms, daring to recklessness on the field of battle, swifter than the eagle, stronger than the lion. Yet he was tender as a woman, true to his friend, so capable of inspiring attachment that his armor bearer would face an army at his side, so tenacious of his principles that he clung to his father's fallen fortunes, even though he had suffered from that father all that jealousy could suggest of bitter insult and murderous hate.

It was no child's play that Jonathan undertook in the sacred name of friendship. And he probably was prepared for the outburst that followed his manly protest for his absent friend. On the first feast day, Saul noticed David's absence but said nothing. On the second, however, when David's seat was still vacant, he turned sharply on his son Jonathan and asked the reason: "Wherefore cometh not the son of Jesse to meat, neither yesterday, nor today?" Jonathan instantly made the preconcerted answer about David's desire to see his family, indicating that he had himself given permission for David's absence. This identification of himself with David brought on Jonathan an outburst of ungovernable rage. Saul's fury knew no bounds. With stinging allusion to Jonathan's mother as the source of his son's perversity, with taunts that were intended to instill into Jonathan's heart the poison that was working in his own, with demands that David should be instantly brought and put to death—the monarch clearly showed his extreme hatred and determination that the son of Jesse should no longer tarry above ground. Jonathan made one vain attempt to reason with the furious monarch, but he might as well have tried to arrest the swelling of Jordan in the time of flood. In a paroxysm of ungovernable passion, the king cast his spear at him to smite him. Then Jonathan knew that they must prepare for the worst and left the table in a fierce anger, being grieved for his friend because his father had done him shame.

Never be ashamed to own a friend. Do not count him your friend whose name you are ashamed to mention and with whose company you blush to be identified. When you have entered into an alliance with another soul whom you love as Jonathan loved David, dare to stand up for him at all cost to your comfort and relations with those who do not know your friend as you know him. It is a noble thing when a man or woman in circles where fashion and pride rule dares to take the part of some unpopular righteous cause, of some maligned but holy servant of God, of some unpolished but sterling associate. This stamps the confessor with the guinea-die of native worth. It is easier to storm a fort than to withstand the covert sneer and the contemptuous look.

But there is something still nobler, when one dares in any company to confess his loyalty to the Lord Jesus. Like David, Jesus Christ is now in obscurity and disrepute. His name is not popular, His gospel is misrepresented, and His followers are subjected to rebuke and scorn. These are days when to stand up for anything more than mere conventional religion must cost something. For this very reason, let us never flinch, but as we trust that He will confess our name before His Father and the angels, let us not be ashamed of His. Jonathan's arrows showed that he did not hesitate to stand alone for David. Let our own words assure Him, who is just now hidden, that we will bear scorn, abuse, and death for His dear name.

Never be ashamed to speak up for the cause of truth. How often the spirit of expediency whispers in our ear: "Let it pass. Wait till the dinner is done. Do not make a spectacle of yourself. Take an opportunity for private confrontation. Sit still, be pleasant, we will see what can be done presently." Jonathan took the nobler course. The dainties were on his plate, but he would not touch them. The cup was in his hand, but he would not place it to his lips. His father was before him, with his claims on his reverence and respect as the king, having the power of life and death in his mouth. But Jonathan dared not hold his peace. Had it been simply a question of his own position or respect, of mere politeness, civility, courtesy due to age, he would have been the first to put his hand upon his mouth and be silent. But it was a question of truth, righteousness, and justice.

If Jonathan were to be still, the very stones in the wall would cry out against him, and he would forfeit the respect of his own conscience.

But it may be asked, Is it not improper to force our opinions among those who are older and more learned than ourselves? Yes, but there is all the difference in the world between opinions spun like cobwebs from the brain or caught up at secondhand and those great basic principles of truth, morality, and right that are witnessed to by conscience. When you stand up for these, you do not seek to exalt your own goodness or win an advantage but simply seek to lift the standard from being trampled in the mud. Let the arrows witness to the simplicity and fervor of your allegiance to whatever is lovely and of good report.

THE ARROWS SPOKE OF IMMINENT DANGER

"Jonathan knew that it was determined of his father to slay David" (1 Samuel 20:33). As the lad ran, Jonathan shot an arrow beyond him: "And as soon as the lad was gone, David arose out of a place toward the south, and fell on his face to the ground, and bowed himself three times: and they kissed one another, and wept one with another, until David exceeded" (1 Samuel 20:41). There was no need for Jonathan to enter into explanations; David knew that "the LORD had sent him away" (1 Samuel 20:22).

"The arrows are beyond thee." You have hoped against hope. You have tried to keep your position. You have done your duty, pleaded your cause, sought the intercession of your friends, prayed, wept, agonized. But it is all in vain. The arrow's flight proves that you must go wherever you may. Behind you is the sunny morning, before you an ominous sky. Behind you is the blessed enjoyment of friendship, wife, home, royal favor, and popular adulation; before you is an outcast's life. The heart clings to the familiar and beloved. But the message of those arrows cannot be resisted. There is no alternative but to tear yourself away, take your life in your hand, and go forth, though you know not where. But take these thoughts for your comfort.

There are things we never leave behind. David had an inalienable possession in the love of his friend, in the devotion of the people, in the memory of God's goodness, in his experience of God's delivering care, in the sense of the divine presence that was ever beside him, and in the psalms, which he had already made for himself as well as for the world. There are threads woven into the fabric of our life that can never be extracted or obliterated.

There is a divine purpose determining our course. To the lad there was but royal sport in the flight of the arrow. "What are you doing, my little fellow?" "I am picking up the prince's arrows. We generally go for game, but he is playing at it today." That was all he knew. How little did he understand the purpose of his master and still less realize that each flitting arrow was, so to speak, taken from God's quiver and directed by His hand. There is no chance in a good man's life. Let us recognize the providence of the trivial. Let us believe that behind the arrow's flight there is the loving purpose of our heavenly Father. *He* is sending us away.

The going forth is necessary to secure greater happiness than we leave. Had David lingered in the palace, his life would have been forfeited, and he would have missed all the glory and bliss with which his cup ran over in later years. This was the way to the throne. Only thus could the sentence whispered in his ear by Samuel years before be realized. This mountain pass, with its jagged flints, was the path to the happy valley. The nest was stirred up that he might acquire powers of flight. The trellis work was taken down that the plant might stand alone.

Follow the arrow's flight then beyond the warm circle in which you have so long been sheltered, beyond the southland to the icy north, beyond the known to the unknown. Like another Abraham, go into the land that God will show you. Like another Columbus, turn your prow in the wake of the setting sun. Let David's assurance be yours: "Thou wilt not leave my soul in hell; neither wilt thou suffer thine Holy One to see corruption. Thou wilt shew me the path of life" (Psalm 16:10–11).

THE ARROWS TAUGHT THAT HUMAN LOVE MUST SUFFER SEPARATION

This was the last meeting of these two noble hearts for a long time. Indeed, the friends met only once more, shortly before Jonathan's death. They had realized that this must be so. The soul of Jonathan, especially, seems to have been overcast with the impression that their happy friendship would never again be renewed. Therefore he pledged David with that pathetic vow to be faithful to his seed and to remember their love when all his enemies had been cut off. "Go in peace," Jonathan said, finally, as though he could no longer bear the awful anguish of that parting, "forasmuch as we have sworn both of us in the name of the LORD, saying, The LORD be between me and thee, and between my seed and thy seed for ever" (1 Samuel 20:42). Then David arose and departed to become a fugitive and an outlaw, liable at any moment to capture and violent death. Jonathan returned thoughtfully and sadly to the palace, where he must spend the rest of his life in contact with one who had no sympathy for his noble sentiments, who had outraged his tenderest sensibilities.

These are the hours that leave scars on hearts and whiten the hair. The world in its rush is so unconscious of all the tragedies that are taking place around. Young hearts suffer till they can suffer no more. Aged ones cannot forget. Years after some scene like this, eyes will film with tears as it is recalled. But Christ comes to us in these dark moments, as of old to the disciples, on whom had broken the full import of their Master's approaching departure. "Let not your heart be troubled....believe also in me" (John 14:1). There is no comfort like this. To believe that He is ordering each detail, to know that love is prompting each action of His hand and each thought of His mind, to lie back on His bosom and utterly trust Him—there is nothing like this to bridge the yawning gulf of separation, with its turbid, rushing stream beneath.

10

1 Samuel 21; Psalm 56

ALMOST GONE

But oh, whatever of worst ill betide,
Choose not this manner to evade your woe:
Be true to God; on Him in faith abide,
And sure deliverance you at length shall know.
It may be that some path His hand will show
To your dear earthly hopes; or He will shape
For you at length a way of glad escape.

Trench

*I*t is not easy to walk with God. The air that beats around the Himalaya heights of divine fellowship is rare and hard to breathe. Human feet tire after a little. And faith, hard put to it, is inclined to give up the effort of keeping step with the divine pace. Such was what David found, and there came in his experience a terrible lapse, the steps and consequences of which, together with his recovery, must occupy us for a space.

THE STEPS OF DAVID'S DECLENSION

The first sign of what was impending was David's remark to Jonathan that there was but a step between himself and death (1 Samuel 20:3). Evidently his faith was beginning to falter, for nothing could have been more definite than the divine assurances that he was to be king. He looked at God through the mist of circumstances that certainly to the eye of reason were sufficiently threatening, instead of looking at circumstances through the golden haze of God's very present help. The winds and waves were more daunting than the promise of God was inspiring. The javelin of Saul intercepted the remembrance of the hour—now rapidly receding into the distance—when he had received the anointing oil at the hand of Samuel. The apostle John says that it is not enough to receive the anointing once; it must *abide* in us, for this was the characteristic of our Lord, that the baptism saw the Spirit descending and *abiding upon* Him. But perhaps David relied too absolutely on what he had received and neglected the daily renewal of the heavenly empowering (John 1:33–34; 1 John 3:24).

Next, David adopted a strategy that was not worthy of him or of his great and mighty Friend. This was a further descent from the high place of heavenly fellowship and testimony. God is light, and light is truth, and those who walk with Him must put off the works of darkness and put on the armor of light, walking as children of the day.

Late in the afternoon of the day preceding the weekly Sabbath, the king's son-in-law arrived with a mere handful of followers at the little town of Nob, situated among the hills about five miles to the south of Gibeah. It was a peaceful secluded spot, apart from the highways of commerce and war, as became the character and calling of its inhabitants, who were engaged in the service of the sanctuary. Four score and six persons who wore the linen ephod dwelt there with their wives, their children, their oxen, asses, and sheep. Into the tranquil course of existence in that holy and retired spot hardly a ripple came from the storms that swept the outer world. There was certainly no provision made to repel invading footsteps, for no weapon was found there but the sword of Goliath, deposited years before as a trophy by the youthful champion. Probably the great annual convocations had fallen into disuse, and the path to the simple sanctuary was trodden only by occasional visitors, such as Doeg, who came to pay their vows or be cleansed from ceremonial pollution. There was evidently no attempt made to prepare for large numbers. The slim budget of the priests only just sufficed for them, and the presence of two or three additional strangers completely overbalanced the slender food supply. There were not five loaves of common bread to spare.

It was necessary to answer the questions and allay the suspicions of the priest, and David did this by pleading the urgency of the mission on which his royal master had sent him. He led Ahimelech to suppose that his young attendants and he had been at least three days on this expedition and that the king had specially insisted on privacy and secrecy. He assured him that a large escort awaited him at a distance. But a chill struck to his heart while making these excuses to the simpleminded priest and enlisting his cooperation in the matter of provisions and arms, as he saw the dark visage of Doeg, the Edomite, "the chiefest of the herdmen that belonged to Saul" (1 Samuel 21:7).

David knew that the whole story would be mercilessly repeated to the vindictive and vengeful monarch. Uneasiness for his unsuspecting host and fear for himself filled his heart, and as soon as the Sabbath was over, he left the spot and with all haste struck across the hills in a southwesterly direction until he cut the deep depression of the valley of Elah, where he had achieved the great victory of his life. Its aspect was strangely altered, its only tenants then being the wild creatures of earth and sky. Ten miles beyond lay the proud Philistine city of Gath, which at that time had sent its champion forth in all the pride of his stature and strength. Behind, David had left an implacable foe. What worse fate could await him at Gath than that which threatened him each hour he lingered within the limits of Judah! He therefore resolved to make the plunge, probably hoping that the shepherd lad of years ago would not be recognized in the mature warrior or that the Philistines would be glad to have his aid in their wars against his countrymen.

Not a little to his dismay, and perhaps on account of Goliath's sword hanging at his belt, David was instantly recognized. The servants of Achish recalled the refrain that had already awakened the jealousy of Saul. David was instantly regarded with hatred, as having slain his ten thousands. His hands had been soaked in Philistine blood, and his fortunes had come at the expense of bereaved hearts and homes throughout the Philistine territory. Here, however, was an easy opportunity of avenging all. By some means, David became aware of the evil impression at court and saw the immense peril in which he stood of imprisonment or execution. He saved himself by descending to the unworthy subterfuge of counterfeiting the behavior of a madman, drumming on the doors of the city gate and allowing his spittle to fall down upon his beard. His device succeeded, and Achish dismissed him with the humorous remark to his servants that he had already madmen enough around him. This certainly was one of the least dignified episodes in David's varied life, very unworthy of God's anointed. The shame was that there would have been no need for it had he not departed through unbelief from the living God.

THE PSALM OF THE SILENT DOVE

At first sight, we are startled with the apparently irreconcilable discrepancy between the scenes we have just described and the fifty-sixth psalm, the inscription of which associates it with them. But there is no reason to doubt the accuracy of that ancient note, which is probably due to David's hand and is at least as old as the first arrangement of the psalter in the days of Solomon.

Closer inspection will reveal many resemblances between the singer's circumstances and his touching words. We are reminded that beneath much that is unworthy and contemptible there may burn a true devotion, an eager yearning after God, a soul of good amid things evil. The cursory spectator would not have supposed that this dissembling madman was meditating thoughts that were to express for all generations the most implicit faith, the sincerest trust. But so it was.

The major part of this exquisite psalm consists of two stanzas, culminating in the same refrain. The remainder is full of hope and praise and the expression of the joy with which the psalmist anticipates walking before God in the light of life.

First Stanza (1–4). David turns to God from man, to the divine mercy from the close ranks of his foes who, surging around him, threaten to engulf and swallow him up. He counts himself as a lonely dove far from its native woods. His heart trembles and misgives amid the many who fight proudly against him. Yet he contrasts fear with faith, arguing with himself as to the baselessness of his dread and contrasting man's fleshy might with God's supreme power. Thus he climbs up out of the weltering waves, his feet on a rock, a new song in his mouth, the burden of which is, "I will not fear." Oh, happy soul, who has learned to take your stand on God as your rock and fortress!

Second Stanza (5–9) Again, David is in the depths. The returning wave has sucked him back. His boast changed to a moan, his challenge to complaint. Never a moment of intermission from the wrestling of his words, not a glint of respite from the hostility of their thoughts, not a step that is not watched by the scrutiny of those who lie in wait for his soul. He wanders fitfully from shelter to shelter. His tears fall thick and fast. His enemies are as numerous as the hairs of his head. Ah, soul! Is this your voice that but a moment ago was resonant with praise? Alas for you! Yet as we commiserate, we hear the voice of faith again ringing out the positive assurance, "I know that God is for me," and again the old refrain comes back:

> In God will I praise his word:
> in the LORD will I praise his word.
> In God have I put my trust:
> I will not be afraid
> What man can do unto me (vv. 10–11).

Third Stanza (10–13). There is no further relapse. David's heart is fixed, trusting the Lord; the vows of God are upon his head. He looks back upon the dark abyss into which his soul had nearly fallen and knows that he is delivered from it forever. As the morning breaks, he sees the mark of his footprints to the edge of the precipice and recognizes the divine power and grace that have delivered his feet from falling. And now, as once again he regains the sunny uplands that he had so shamefully renounced in his flight from Gibeah to Nob, from Nob to Gath, from Gath to feigned insanity, he is sure that henceforth he will walk before God in the light of life. Truth, purity, and joy shall be the garments of his soul.

In the extreme anguish of those hours at Gath, when David thought that the torch of his life would go out in the dark waters of Philistine hatred, the backslider had returned to God, had caught the rope by which to spring from the abyss into the light, and once again sat, as a child at home, anointed with oil, with a table spread before him in the presence of his enemies.

THE CONSEQUENCES TO AHIMELECH

A child of God may be forgiven and restored, yet the consequences of his sin may involve sufferings to many innocent lives. So it was in this instance. It happened shortly after, when Saul was sitting under the tamarisk tree in Ramah with his spear in his hand

and his servants around him. He was endeavoring to excite their sympathy by enumerating the supposed wrongs he had suffered at the hand of David, and Doeg took the opportunity of ingratiating himself in the royal favor by narrating what he had seen at Nob. He carefully withheld the unsuspecting innocence and ignorance of the priest and so told the tale as to make it appear that Ahimelech and his house were accomplices with David's action and perhaps bent on helping David to gain supreme power. It was in vain that Ahimelech protested his innocence, enumerated David's services, referred to the many occasions on which David had sought his help, persisted in the avowal of his ignorance of the quarrel between Saul and his son-in-law. Before night fell, the white vesture of the priests was soaked with their blood, and every living thing in the little mountain town was smitten with the edge of the sword. By one ruthless act, the entire priestly community was exterminated.

There was but one survivor, for Abiathar escaped, carrying the ephod in his hands. And one day, to his horror, David beheld the dishevelled, blood-smeared form of the priest as he sped breathless and panic-stricken up the valley of Elah to find shelter with the outlaw band in the cave of Adullam. We shall hear of him again.

Meanwhile, let children of God beware! Sin is bitter to the conscience of the sinner and in its consequences upon others. Let us walk carefully, watchfully, prayerfully, exercising our consciences repeatedly to see whether there be any swerving from the path of strict integrity. We need to beware lest seeds be scattered beyond recovery, to bear bitter harvests in the lives of those who, through their mysterious union with ourselves, are inextricably involved in the consequences of our deeds.

11

THE CAVE
OF ADULLAM

For good ye are and bad, and like to coins—
Some true, some light; but every one of you
Stamp'd with the image of the king.

Tennyson

With a very thankful heart for God's delivering mercy, David left Gath and hastily recrossed the frontier, finding himself again in the kingdom of Saul. His life, however, was in great jeopardy, and he did not dare expose himself to the royal jealousy. To return to court was impossible, and he did not care to incur the risk of involving his relatives in his troubles by seeking shelter at Bethlehem. There was apparently no alternative but to adopt the life of a fugitive and wanderer amid the hills of Judah with which his shepherd life had made him so familiar.

Two miles up the valley of Elah from Gath there is a labyrinth of hills and valleys, deeply honeycombed with caves. One of these caves, near the ancient Canaanitish city of Adullam and named after it, afforded David for a considerable period the shelter of

71

which he was in search. It is described as a dark vault, the entrance of which is a low window in the perpendicular face of the cliff. Its position made it possible for him to cross from one country to another, as the occasion required. To this cave fled David's whole family, dreading, no doubt, the violence of Saul's hatred. Then also came those in distress and in debt and the discontented, and David became captain over them.

We need not now expand on David's filial love, which traversed the entire distance from Adullam to Moab in order to secure a safe place for his father and mother, who were probably too aged to stand the hardships and dangers of his fugitive life. Suffice it to say that his petition was readily granted by the king of Moab, perhaps on account of some pride in the Moabite blood that flowed in the veins of the young Hebrew warrior. But that double journey, first to secure the shelter and then to escort the aged couple there, reveals a pleasing trait in David's character. There was no lack of obedience to the commandment to honor your father and mother. It is, however, upon the cave and the more motley group of David's supporters that we will focus.

The Cave And Its Lessons

There can be no doubt that the Holy Ghost, in the detailed narration of these experiences in David's life, wants us to trace an analogy between David's history and that of the Lord Jesus in his present rejection and banishment from the throne of the world. The parallel is as specific as it is instructive.

A rejected king was on the throne. Though anointed by Samuel, Saul by disobedience had forfeited his right to reign and effectually nullified the effect of the sacred empowering as we may do also. The sentence of removal had been pronounced and awaited its execution at the appropriate moment. Similarly, the dark fallen spirit, Satan, was once an anointed cherub who was set on the holy mountain of God and perfect in his ways from the day that he was created until unrighteousness was found in him. It appears that he derives the title that our Lord gave him of "prince of this world" (John 12:31) from his original appointment as God's vicegerent and representative; but in his fall, Satan forfeited his glorious position, and man was created as his substitute to take his place. "What is man?... Thou...didst set him over the works of thy hands" (Hebrews 2:6–7).

That power is not yet exercised by man—"we see not yet all things put under him" (Hebrews 2:8). But we see it in the person of the Son of Man, who is already "crowned with glory and honour" (Hebrews 2:9).

In the meantime, Satan still holds the throne of the world. Countless times has Satan cast his javelin at the King after God's own heart. In the temptation and in Gethsemane, Satan would fain have pinned Jesus to the wall. All through the present age, Satan has been doing his worst to exterminate the incipient hidden Kingdom of Jesus, though he knows that God has destined it to take the place of his own. But all his attempts must fail. As Saul fell on the field of Gilboa, so the prince of darkness shall be finally cast into the bottomless pit.

David's kingdom was hidden. It was a true kingdom, though in mystery, veiled in the darkness of Adullam's cave and concealed in the labyrinth of valleys and hills. In essence, David had fallen into the ground to die, that he might not abide alone but bring forth much fruit. It is a mysterious process through which the little seed passes in the winter when it surrenders itself to the destructive forces that lie in wait and seize on its tender fabric. "Exposed to wintry winds, trodden under the feet of those who drive the rake and harrow over it; buried out of sight and left alone, as if cast out by God and man to endure the slow process of a daily dissolution; then melted by rains and heats until its form is marred, and it seems useless to either God or man." Such was the experience of David, and it was also the experience of that divine King. Jesus fell into the mystery of forsakenness on the cross and the mystery of rejection in the grave, and His person and Kingdom are now altogether hidden from the world of men.

The day is close at hand when the Lord, who is hidden until the time of the restitution of all things, shall be manifested with His saints and take to Himself His great power and reign. The pearl that He won from the ocean caves shall be worn on His brow. The treasure for which He bought the field of the world shall be spread forth for the admiration of the universe. The army that He has constituted from such unpromising materials shall follow Him on white horses in radiant array. In the meanwhile, His Kingdom is "in mystery."

David and his followers were in separation. Driven out from the camp of Israel, they had no alternative. With the feasts and pageants, the counsels and decisions, the nation's politics and foreign wars of Saul, they had no immediate connection, although the cave of Adullam could not but exert an important indirect influence on the whole realm. The destiny of an exile, the path of the wanderer and stranger, were measured out to David and those who were willing to share his lot. His way to the throne lay through multiplied difficulties and sorrows. Though David must have prized the freer air, the sense of liberty, the deliverance from the heartless and godless etiquette of the palace, there must have been a perpetual sadness and loneliness in his soul.

The true King of men is still outside human politics and society. We cannot have Him and them. Those who desire to be His subjects and to share the rewards and glories of those coming days, when He shall have dominion from sea to sea and from the river to the ends of the earth, must go out to Him without the camp, willing to forsake all that they have and be counted the offscouring of all things (Hebrews 13:13).

David was content to await God's time. Whatever provocation Saul gave, David never retaliated. However easy the opportunity of gaining an advantage over his vindictive pursuer, David never availed himself of it. He was prepared to wait God's time and to receive supreme power in God's way. He quieted himself as a weaned child. His perpetual refrain is recorded in his own words: "My soul, wait thou only upon God; for my expectation is from him" (Psalm 62:5). It was as though he sat down in patience and submission till God made his foes the footstool of his feet and set him as His king on His holy hill of Zion. It is in this manner, through these passing centuries, that our Savior is waiting. Now is the time of the Kingdom and *patience* of Jesus Christ. And here is the patience of the saints, while the eager expectation and yearning of the whole creation are waiting for the manifestation of the sons of God. Ourselves also, who have the firstfruits of the Spirit, even we ourselves groan within ourselves, waiting for the adoption to come, the redemption of our body. For by hope we were saved; but hope that is seen is not hope, for who hopes for what he sees? But if we hope for what we do not see, then we wait for it with patience.

THE CAVE AND ITS INMATES

The tidings of David's return to Judah and of his retreat in the shelter of the cave spread swiftly and mysteriously throughout the whole land, and those who were sorely pressed by misery, poverty, and bitterness of soul began to flock around him. The young leader soon found himself at the head of four hundred men, who formed a very motley crew! For the few who were loyal to David there were superior numbers of those who were full of their own grievances and eager only for the righting of wrongs. The sacred historian says that their faces were like the faces of lions and that they were as swift as deer upon the mountains. But their tempers were probably turbulent and fierce, requiring all; the grace and tact and states-manship that the young ruler was capable of to reduce them to dis-cipline and order. It was surely no small feat to so organize such a diverse group that they became the nucleus of the greatest army of their time and carried the national boundaries of Israel to the fullest limits it ever reached.

We must not think of David at this time in his career as a ban-dit or a plunderer, but rather should think of him as the improvisor of a frontier guard to defend the land against the Amalekites and Philistines, who were perpetually raiding the land at the time of har-vest and sweeping away the farmers' toils. Thus, David became the benefactor and defender of his people, though exiled from them. In the common talk of the time, his men and he were described as a wall to the great sheep masters and agriculturists of southern Judah, "both by night and day" (1 Samuel 25:16).

It is impossible not to turn from David to Jesus, who, though cast out from the scheme of this world and its prince, is ever gath-ering into His Kingdom the poor and outcast, the leper and sinner, the blind and bruised and brokenhearted, those who are in distress, in debt, and discontented, and making them into soldiers who shall win the world for Himself.

Did these wild, rough soldiers find a new center for their life in David? We have found a new object in the Lord Jesus, for whom to live is life indeed and for whom to die is gain.

Did this new center draw them away from attachment and asso-ciation with the decadent kingdom of Saul? Our oneness with the living Savior has made us unworldly by making us *other* worldly. We have cast in our lot with Him, becoming citizens of the new Jerusalem and being glad to confess ourselves strangers and pil-grims on this earth.

Did they put off the manners and customs of their old life, allowing the shuttle of love and devotion to weave the fabric of a new character? We have put off the old man with his doings and have put on the new man, which is being renewed unto knowledge after the image of Him who created him.

Did they love David for removing their discontent, alleviating their distress, and relieving them from the disorder and anxiety of their existence? Much more should we love Jesus, who has done infinitely more for us than even David did for his poor followers. Jesus has paid our debts with His precious blood, relieved us from our creditors by meeting them Himself, clothed us in His perfect beauty, allayed our sorrows, calmed and stilled our souls.

Did the attachment between David and his followers grow with the years, cementing them in a fellowship that was the result of sharing common dangers—the bivouac fire by night, the toilsome march by day, the brush with the foe? What an incentive for us to seek a fellowship with our blessed Lord that shall grow closer for every day of trial we share with Him!

THE CAVE AND ITS SONG

Many allusions connect the thirty-fourth psalm with the cave of Adullam. It was there that the little host needed the encamping angel, there that the young lions roared as they ranged the wilds in search of food, there also that God's care was perpetually laid under requisition to protect the bones of the fugitives lest they should be broken by falling down the crags (vv. 7, 10, 20).

We can imagine the leader one evening, when the anxieties and fatigues of the day were over, gathering his troops around him with the words, "Come, ye children, hearken unto me: I will teach you the fear of the LORD" (v. 11). Then, in quick succession, the three exhortations: "O magnify the LORD with me," (v. 3)... "O taste and see that the LORD is good:" (v. 8)... "0 fear the LORD, ye his saints" (v. 9). Then, perhaps, from all their voices came the full chorus: "The LORD redeemeth the soul of his servants: and none of them that trust in him shall be desolate" (v. 22).

The soul that is living a separated life, with sin judged, forsaken, and forgiven behind it, may count on these four:

Deliverance—even in the midst of difficulties and perplexities that have been caused by its own misdeeds (w. 4, 7, 17, 19).

Enlightenment—for what the dawn is to the weary watcher, that God will be to the soul who has long groped in the dark if only the face is turned towards His (v. 5).

Perfect provision—so that it shall lack nothing that it really needs (v. 10).

The sense of God's closeness—nearer than the nearest, more real than the presence or absence of any (v. 18).

If in that cave, with so many things to distract him, compelled to spend every hour in the presence of his men, David was able to realize the presence of God, how much more possible it must be for us! And once that is realized, all the conditions of the best life are fulfilled.

What makes the difference between the dull and gray of winter and the beauty of the spring? Is it not that the sun is closer and nature knows it and assimilates his glorious color?

So, backslider! broken heart! contrite spirit! Do not look back on past failure and shortcoming or stand in dread of recurring sin, but look up and away to the face of Jesus. Do not, I pray you, live on the dying, but live on the living side. Dwell in the secret place of the Most High. Abide in the house of the Lord all the days of your life. Enter with boldness the Holiest, to remain there. Ask the Holy Spirit to enable you to realize the constant presence of God. Say to yourself often throughout each day, even when you do not feel it, "You are here; you are here." Make a home for yourself in the sense of God's nearness. Oh, taste and see the sweetness of such a life!

It was thus that Jesus thought of His Father, and it is thus that you will realize the happiest, strongest experiences possible to the saints. "The LORD is nigh unto them that are of a broken heart; and saveth such as be of a contrite spirit" (Psalm 34:18).

12

1 Samuel 23:6; Psalm 27

THE
WHITE STONE

Will not God impart His light
To them that ask it?—Freely—'tis His joy,
His glory, and His nature, to impart;
But to the proud, uncandid, insincere,
Or negligent inquirer, not a spark.

Cowper

*I*t is not perfectly clear where David was when he was joined by Abiathar. If we consider the time, we are disposed to fix the massacre of the priests shortly after David's flight to Gath. In that case, Abiathar must have come to him while David was in his first prolonged hiding place in the cave of Adullam. It is on this supposition that we have already sketched the fugitive Abiathar making his approach, breathless and dishevelled.

If, however, we judge by the position given to the incident on the page of Scripture, we should be disposed to locate it in the forest of Hareth—a tract of country a little to the south of Adullam and not far from Hebron. The prophet Gad, who had recently joined David and was destined to share the fortunes of the young refugee's long career, living to chronicle his entire history, seems to have advised this exchange. In the case of pursuit, the open country would be safer than a cave that might be closed at the entrance and become a death trap (1 Samuel 22:5; 1 Chronicles 21:9; 29:29).

On the other hand, 1 Samuel 23:6 suggests that Abiathar came to David at Keilah. But good authorities question the authenticity of the words "to Keilah," especially as the Septuagint reads: "It came to pass, when Abiathar the son of Ahimelech fled to David, then he went down with David to Keilah, having the ephod in his hand." If this were so, the inquiries mentioned in the previous verses (1–5) would have been made through the Urim and Thummin, as was the custom in those days.

There is no need to delay further in the attempt to fix what is of no material importance. Our present purpose is rather to bring into prominence David's lifelong habit of waiting upon God for direction and guidance. It is instructive and stimulating to notice that the successive steps of David's career were taken after very definite waiting upon God. It was as though the advice he gives us in Psalm 27:14, which dates from this period, was the outcome of his own deepest experience and practice:

> Wait on the LORD:
> be of good courage, and he shall strengthen thine heart:
> wait, I say, on the LORD.

The expression of the psalmist's soul in this psalm, in his practice as delineated by the historian, and in the lessons we see in his life may well be incorporated into our daily walk—such is the trend of our thought.

The Psalmist's Attitude And Desire

There are several items of internal evidence that connect Psalm 27 with this period of David's life. David's fortunes were as dark as the interior of Adullam's cave; therefore he spoke of God as his light. David was in daily peril; therefore it was his comfort that God would be his salvation. Jehovah was more really his stronghold than even that fortress of rock. Evildoers might come upon him to eat up his flesh, but they would stumble and fall, as Goliath had done in that very ravine. Hosts might encamp against David, but his heart would not fear. War might rise against him, but in this would he be confident. David would be hid in the covert of God's tent from all pursuit or be set upon a rock at an elevation inaccessible to his foes. True, he had no longer the safe place of the old home in Bethlehem; in that sense, his father and mother had forsaken him. But God would gather him and be father and mother both (v. 10).

The further references to his extreme need and anguish, to the necessity of being led in a plain path, to the false witnesses who had risen against him and who breathed out cruelty—an allusion that may be very well accounted for by Abiathar's account of Doeg's treacherY—combine to associate this lovely and endearing psalm with David's residence in the cave. It is just such a cry as must frequently have broken from his heart in those sad and dark days. How often must the splintered rocks around have heard David's strong cryings and tears, witnessing the awful swoon of his soul, nigh unto death, as he looked down on the abyss from which he was hardly delivered. David could not forget that by his recent lapse at Gath he had given cause for God to hide His face from him, to leave him, and to put him away in anger. But David pleads that through all those bitter passages of his life he "believed to see the goodness of the LORD in the land of the living" (v. 13). And he comforts himself by the reflection that He who sustained his soul with the blessed hope could not fail to realize the vision with which He had allured the wanderer back to Himself.

The main objection against the supposition that the psalm dates from this period of David's life arises from his mention of the Lord's house, tabernacle, and temple. Still, this is not conclusive. We met with the germ of the same thought in Psalm 23, where the shepherd-minstrel desired to dwell in the house of the Lord forever. As young as he was, it is unlikely that David would have desired seclusion for the rest of his days in the narrow limits of Levitical service. This had been an unwholesome craving, entirely out of keeping with his heroic soul. Surely, then, the desire for an abiding place in the house of the Lord—which was the wish of his shepherd days, of his cave experiences, and of his exile when fleeing from Absalom—can be interpreted only as referring to an intimacy of divine fellowship, a constant flow of blessed communication that should supply guidance and direction in all the dark and tortuous pathways of his history.

What fresh and vivid meaning invests his words when read

under this light! He desired to abide in communion with God and to have face-to-face conversation with Him, as the priests within the precincts of the shrine at Nob. David wished to be able at any moment to inquire of the holy oracle. It was his choice to live so near to God that whenever he heard the divine summons, though in whispers too faint for ordinary ears, "Seek ye my face," he might be near enough to hear it and reply, "Thy face, Lord, will I seek."

HIS HABITUAL PRACTICE

When the trembling priest had told his story, David addressed to him the words that have a sweet application when placed in the lips of Christ. It is thus that our outcast King, driven beyond the camp, receives each fugitive soul that has recourse to Him: "Abide thou with me," He says; "fear not: for he that seeketh my life seeketh thy life: but with me thou shalt be in safeguard" (1 Samuel 22:23).

The special reason that made David glad to welcome Abiathar was that he brought with him, rescued from the sack of the little town, the sacred ephod, within which were the sacred Urim and Thummin. The words signify "Light and Perfection"; it is by no means certain what they refer to.

The most probable explanation is that the high priest's inner garment was a white linen tunic. Over this tunic the high priest wore a blue robe, and above this, the ephod, made of white-twined linen, inwrought with blue and purple and scarlet and gold. To this was affixed the breastplate, in which were twelve precious stones, corresponding to the twelve tribes of Israel. In this breastplate, perhaps part of it or attached to it, were probably either one or two very beautiful and resplendent diamonds, through which God manifested His will. If the priest brought a question to Him that was answered no, the light in these precious stones dimmed. If, on the contrary, the answer was yes, the stones flashed with splendor.

It was obviously a great gain to David to have at hand this priceless method of communication between Jehovah and himself. Already Gad was with him as the representative of the prophetic office; now Abiathar and the ephod represented the most precious prerogative of the priesthood. By one or other of these, and probably in these earlier days especially by the latter, he was able at any moment to know the will of God.

When tidings come that the Philistines are plundering Keilah,

David dares not pursue until he has asked the Lord. If the cowardly townspeople propose to betray their deliverer, he dares not leave the city until he has received divine direction to go. In one of the most awful experiences of David's life, when his men spoke of stoning him instead of taking up his cause, David said to Abiathar the priest, "I pray thee, bring me hither the ephod" (1 Samuel 30:7). Then Abiathar brought the ephod to David, and David inquired of the Lord. Long after he had become the acknowledged king of the land, in his conflicts with the Philistines he was careful to inquire of the Lord as to the very method of attack (2 Samuel 5:17–25).

Evidently this was the holy practice of David's life: to wait on God, quieting the fever of his soul and compelling the crowd of impetuous thoughts to be suspended until time had been given for the clear disclosure of the divine purpose and plan. Like the child who dares not take one step alone, like the traveler in a strange country who is utterly dependent on his guide, so David lifted up his soul for the supreme direction that only God can give and to whom the future is as clearly defined as the past and from whom no secrets can be hid.

The Lesson For Ourselves

When the children of Israel came up out of Egypt, they were led across the desert by the pillar of cloud and fire. After they were settled in their own land, the Urim and Thummin took their place. After a while, this method of determining God's will fell into disuse, and the prophets spoke as they were moved by the Holy Ghost. These, even in the early church, played a very important part in the directing of God's people in His way.

But the voices of the prophets were silenced as the apostolic age came to a close. What is our oracle of appeal? Are godly souls without the means of inquiring of the Lord and receiving His clear direction on the difficult questions perpetually demanding solution? Not so; for in one of the last messages given by the ascended Lord to His Church through the apostle John, it was foretold that he who overcame should receive a *white stone*, and the word *white* means resplendent or lustrous. It may therefore denote a diamond and probably refers to those ancient stones in the high priest's breastplate that dimmed or flashed with the divine oracles. On them the holy name Jehovah was inscribed in mystic characters. Similarly, it is said that on the white stone, received by every believer who over-comes in the spiritual conflict against sin and the world, a new name will be written, unknown except to him who received it (Revelation 2:17).

In other words, each child of God has his own Urim and Thummin stone, which I take to mean a conscience void of offense, a heart cleansed in the blood of Christ, a spiritual nature that is per-vaded and filled by the Holy Spirit of God.

When we are in doubt or difficulty, when many voices urge this course or the other, when prudence utters one advice and faith another, let us be still, hushing each intruder, calming ourselves in the sacred hush of God's presence. Let us study His Word in the atti-tude of devout attention. Let us lift up our heart into the pure light of His face, eager only to know what God the Lord shall determine. Before long a very distinct impression will be made, the unmistak-able forthtelling of His secret counsel. It is not wise, in the earlier stages of Christian life, to depend on this alone, but to wait for the corroboration of circumstances. But those who have had many deal-ings with God know well the value of secret fellowship with Him to ascertain His will. The journals of George Fox are full of references to this secret of the Lord, which is with them who fear Him and to whom He shows His covenant.

Are you in difficulty about your way? Go to God with your ques-tion. Get direction from the light of His smile or the cloud of His refusal. If only you will get alone, where the lights and shadows of earth cannot interfere, where the disturbance of self-will does not intrude, where human opinions fail to reach—and if you will dare to wait there in silence and expectation, though all around you insist on immediate decision or action—the will of God will be made clear. And you will have a new name in addition, a new con-ception of God, a deeper insight into His nature and heart of love that shall be for yourself alone—a rapturous experience, to abide your precious blessing forever, the rich reward of those long waiting hours.

13

SONGS BORN OF SORROW

A song of the heart that is broken,
A song of the sighs and the tears.
The sickness, the want, and the sadness
Of the days of our pilgrimage years.

Sweet sings the great choir of sorrow,
The songs of the gladness untold,
To Him on the throne of His glory,
Who wept in the days of old.

H. Sears

*T*he Church owes many of her sweetest hymns to the profound anguish that rung the hearts of her noblest children. The rough feet of trial and pain have stamped, as in the wine press, hearts whose lifeblood is preserved in matchless lyrics. There is no such raw material for songs that live from heart to heart as that furnished by sorrow.

A modern writer has said that the mysterious beauty of music is more wonderful than the abundance of form and color that overspreads the whole of nature. He went on to show that man only develops and liberates the music that is latent in almost all substances, waiting for his coming to give it expression. "Man only develops what was within them, just as the coal that is extracted from the bowels of the earth, when set on fire, merely liberates the heat and light that it received from the sun in the forest." Is not this speechless music—locked within nature, pleading to be let out in song or sound through the agency of man—part of the earnest expectation of the creature that waits for the manifestation of the sons of God?

It is remarkable how many of David's psalms date from those dark and sad days when he was hunted as a partridge upon the mountains. His path may be tracked through the psalms as well as in the sacred narrative of his wanderings. Keilah, Ziph, Maon, Engedi, yielded themes for strains that will live forever. To this gifted singer the power was entrusted of eliciting the music that lay concealed in the least congenial haunts. Is it not strange that these wild desolations are now immortal and that each has contributed chords to the complete music of the soul? We will for a little trace the parallel lines of David's history and song.

A Cluster Of Psalms

Keilah. While sheltering in the forest of Hareth, tidings came of a raid of the Philistines on one of the hapless bordertowns. "Behold, the Philistines fight against Keilah, and they rob the threshingfloors" (1 Samuel 23:1). The year's harvest was at that time spread out for threshing; it was an opportune moment therefore for the plunderer. The labors of the years were being carried off, and the cattle "lifted by Israel's bitter and relentless foe." Wrapped in these tidings there was probably a covert appeal for help from one who had often proved himself a wall of defense on the southern frontier. Saul was too far away, and perhaps too intent on his fancied personal wrongs, to be available for the rapid action that was required. David was caring, energetic, and nearby. The appeal to him was not in vain, especially as it was ratified by the divine voice. He arose and went down from the hill country of Judah into the plains, met the marauders on their return journey, heavily laden with booty and slowed by cattle, and smote the Philistines with a great slaughter. David brought back all the spoil to the rejoicing townsfolk, who, in return for his services, gladly lodged and entertained him and his men.

It was a brief spell of sunshine in a dark and cloudy day and must have been very welcome to the weary little band. To be again in a town that had "gates and bars" was as welcome an exchange to life in the dens and caves of the earth as the comforts of civilization are after the frontier of the Tartar steppes. And this gleam of comfort probably elicited from the minstrel-chieftain Psalm 31: "Blessed be the LORD: for he hath shewed me his marvelous kindness in a strong city" (v. 21).

Ziph. David's stay in Keilah was brought to a close by the tidings, given perhaps by Jonathan, that Saul was preparing an expedition to take him, like a trapped bird, even though the city that sheltered his rival were destroyed in the attempt. These tidings were confirmed through the ephod, by which David appealed to the God of Israel. The further information was communicated that the cowardly and ungrateful townsfolk, when forced to choose between the king and David, would not hesitate to save themselves by surrendering their deliverer. Then David and approximately six hundred men arose and departed out of Keilah, going wherever they could. Perhaps they broke up into small parties, while the leader, with the more intrepid and devoted of his followers, made his way to the neighborhood of Ziph, about three miles south of Hebron.

This was about the lowest ebb in David's fortunes. The king was searching for him every day with a malignity that made it evident that he had come out to seek David's life. Beneath the expressions and formulas of devout religion that he carefully maintained (23:7,21), Saul secretly cherished the resolve of thwarting the divine purpose. Because Saul knew that David would be king over Israel, Jonathan told his friend in a hurried interview about the two noble youths arranged in the wood of Ziph. But this did not abate Saul's determination to take David's life if he could. What a desperate condition his soul had reached as the result of turning itself to its own wild and evil way! And David had every reason to fear the outbursts of the hatred that had in proud defiance even set itself against the will of God.

In addition to this relentless hate, there was the meditated treachery of the Ziphites, who sought to curry favor with the king by betraying David's lurking place. Tidings of their intended falseness came to David, and he moved further south to the wilderness of Maon, where a conical hill gives a far extended view of the surrounding country. But to the spot the men of Ziph directed the king with such deadly accuracy that before they could escape, the little beleaguered band found the hill on which they gathered surrounded by the royal troops, and their escape was rendered impossible.

Well for them that a breathless messenger at this juncture burst in on Saul with the words, "Haste thee, and come; for the Philistines have invaded the land" (1 Samuel 23:27). Then David drew a long sigh of relief and sang Psalm 54: "Save me, O God, by thy name, and judge me by thy strength" (v. 1).

Engedi. From Maon, when the heat of the pursuit was over, David removed his quarters eastward to the strongholds of the wild goat on the shores of the Dead Sea. On the western shore, midway between the north and south, there is a little piece of level ground that is covered with the rich luxuriance of tropical vegetation. It is jealously fenced in by giant cliffs, jutting out into the dark waters of the lake, but its beauty is maintained by a tepid stream that issues from the limestone rock, four hundred feet above the glen. It is said that gray weather-beaten stones mark the site of an ancient city and traces of palms have been discovered encrusted in the limestone. But the tangle of a tropical jungle now reigns supreme. This was David's next resort—Engedi, the haunt of the wild goat—where deep caverns in the steep cliffs and the abundance of water supply furnished two of the most important items in his sparse and frugal program. Here again the psalmist sets his experiences to music in two priceless songs. Psalm 57: "Be merciful unto me, O God,…for my soul trusteth in thee" (v. 1), and Psalm 142: "I cried unto the LORD with my voice; with my voice unto the LORD did I make my supplication" (v. 1).

Wilderness experiences also gave rise to other psalms, all of them marked by a recurrence of the same metaphors borrowed from the wilderness and rocky scenery, the same protestations of innocence, the same appeals for the overshadowing wing of the Most High, and the same delicately worded references to Saul. Among these are Psalms 11, 13, 17, 22, 25, and 64.

SOME CHARACTERISTICS OF THESE PSALMS

We cannot deal with the characteristics in detail, but one or two features arrest the most superficial glance.

Their imagery. Men are as lions. "My soul is among lions: and I lie even among them that are set on fire" (Psalm 57:4). David's soul takes refuge in God, hiding in the shadow of His wings, as he had often seen the eaglets do beneath the broad pinion of the parent bird. God is his rock, and David hides in Him as his fugitive troops hid in the strong deep sides of the cave. David's divine helper will not let his enemies triumph over him. It shall happen to his enemies as so often happened to hunters in those very wilds when they fell down the crumbling sides of pits dug to trap the creatures of the forest. At night David shelters in God; with his psaltery he awakes the dawn. All these psalms are bathed in imagery and metaphors like these.

Their delicate references to Saul. David does not spare his epithets for those who goad the king to murderous hate. The men who watched for his stumbling, who cried "Report it! Report it!", who misrepresented and maligned him are dealt with in no hesitating or mincing tones. But of Saul he says nothing, unless there is a veiled allusion to him in the plural, with which he describes the violent men who sought after his life. There is a mournful allusion to happy days, past forever, when David manifested his profound sympathy for the king's terrible malady, wearing sackcloth on his flesh and humbling his soul with fasting (Psalm 35:13). But there are no words of reproach, no upbraidings, no repayment of hate with hate. In this there is an anticipation of the teaching and spirit of Jesus.

There is a conscious integrity. David's conscience was void of offense toward God and man. If challenged as to his absolute sinlessness, David would have been the first to deprecate anything of the sort. David would have acknowledged that in his rough soldier life he was constantly in need of the propitiating sacrifices that would plead for him with God. But in respect to Saul or to any treachery against Saul or his house or to any crime deserving such treatment as that with which he was threatened, David protested his absolute innocence. He turned confidently to God, with clean hands and pure heart, as one who had not lifted up his soul unto vanity or sworn deceitfully (Psalm 7:3–5).

There is great evidence of suffering. Of all sources of pain, there is none so hard to bear, that stings so sharply and strikes its poison fangs so deeply, as the malevolence of our friends. This is what David suffered from most of all. To his highly sensitive spirit it was the most acute form of torture. Though he was absolutely innocent, though he was willing to give himself to prayer and ministry on their behalf, yet his accusers pursued him with such unrelenting malice: "whose teeth are spears and arrows, and their tongue a sharp sword" (Psalm 57:4).

But his appeal was to God.

> Save me, O God, by thy name,
> and judge me by thy strength....
> Behold, God is mine helper:... (Psalm 54:1,4).

> I will cry unto God most high;
> unto God that performeth all things for me.
> He shall send from heaven, and save me...
> God shall send forth his mercy and truth (Psalm 57:2–3).

> Refuge failed me; no man cared for my soul.
> I cried unto thee, O LORD:
> I said, Thou art my refuge (Psalm 142:4–5).

What depths of pathos lie in these stanzas of petition! David does not seek to retaliate or avenge his wrong but commits himself to Him who judges righteously, assured that the Righteous One will shelter him during the time of trial and ultimately bring out his righteousness as the light and his judgment as the noonday.

If any should read these lines who are unjustly maligned and persecuted, let them rest in the Lord and wait patiently for Him. Some little time may elapse before the hour of deliverance strikes, during which they must wear white robes of stainless innocence and purity (Revelation 6:11). But presently God will arise and lift the poor out of the dust, the needy from the dunghill "to set them among princes, and to make them inherit the throne of glory" (1 Samuel 2:8). For the needy shall not always be forgotten nor the expectation of the poor perish forever.

14

1 Samuel 24, 26; Psalm 42:1

DAVID'S
SELF–RESTRAINT

Wait! for the day is breaking,
Though the dull night be long;
Wait! God is not forsaking
Thy heart. Be strong—be strong.

Wait! 't is the key to pleasure
And to the peace of God;
Oh, tarry thou His leisure—
thy soul shall bear no load.

C. Townsend

*A*s David reviewed his life and recorded his experiences, he was well aware of the innumerable evils that had encompassed him, of the horrible pit and miry clay out of which he had been brought up, and of the many who had sought in vain to destroy his soul, but from all he had been delivered. He dared not attribute his deliverance to the quickness of his ingenuity or the agility of his movements, but to God and God only. Mark his record in Psalm 40 of God's dealings with him as he stands on the eminence of the years and looks down and back:

He inclined unto me, and heard my cry.
He brought me up also out of an horrible pit, out of the miry clay, and set my feet upon a rock, and established my goings.

And *he* hath put a new song in my mouth, even praise unto
our God (vv. 4–3)

And if we further inquire what his attitude was during all these
long and sad experiences, he answers:

I waited patiently for the Lord (v. 1).

In a recent chapter we saw how David waited *on* the Lord, but
there is a clear distinction between this and waiting *for* the Lord,
though in practice they are generally united. We wait *on* the Lord by
prayer and supplication, looking for the indication of His will. We
wait *for* the Lord by patience and submission, looking for the inter-
vention of His hand. It is very needful to learn this lesson of silence,
patience, resignation. And it is interesting to remark on the two incidents in 1 Samuel 24 and 26 how perfectly David had acquired it
and had learned to wait for the Lord.

THE BASIS OF WAITING FOR GOD

There must be a promise or a definite commitment of God on
which we can rest as the unmistakable revelation of His purpose. In
their last meeting in the wood of Ziph, Jonathan had given this to
his friend. He had spoken like a messenger from God. How those
words rang in the weary heart that had drunk them in as the
parched land drinks water! "Fear not," he had said, "for the hand
of Saul my father shall not find thee; and thou shalt be king over
Israel, and I shall be next unto thee" (1 Samuel 23:17). He had even
said that this, too, was Saul's conviction: "that also Saul my father
knoweth" (v. 17).

Besides this, David was conscious of his God-given power and
gift to grasp the helm of the distracted kingdom and guide the sorely
tossed vessel into calmer waters. As all these corroborations of the
original promise came into his heart, David became convinced that
God had a great purpose in his life. He settled it in his own mind
that he would wait patiently for the Lord to do as He had said and
that he would not lift his finger to secure the kingdom for himself.
Jehovah had promised, then He would perform. Whenever the
moment came for him to sit on the throne as the acknowledged king
of his people, it would be from first to last the divine gift and the

divine performance. There should be nothing to hinder God from saying: "I set my king upon my holy hill of Zion" (Psalm 2:6).

TWO NOTABLE INCIDENTS

Engedi. One afternoon, when Saul with three thousand men was in hot pursuit of David amid the wild and tangled rocks of Engedi (1 Samuel 24), a strange incident put him completely in David's power. It was a time of breathless heat, the sunbeams were striking like swords into the deep wadis and ravines, and every living thing had crept away into shelter. For the same reason, or because they desired to elude pursuit, David and his men were in the inmost recesses of an immense cavern. Into that very cave Saul came. Saul's men had gone forward, and the intense solitude and silence within and without threw him off his guard. He lingered a while in the entrance.

These caves are dark as midnight, and the keenest eyes cannot see five paces inward. But for one who has grown accustomed to the dark and is looking toward the entrance, all that takes place in that direction can be observed with perfect distinctness. The blinding glare of the sunshine on the limestone cliffs made Saul more than ever unable to detect the forms that lined the cave, while those inside could perfectly well watch his every movement. How little did the king realize the intense interest with which he was being watched by six hundred pairs of eyes, and the peril to which he was exposed! The whole band was thrilled with excitement.

Now was the opportunity for David to end their wanderings and hardships by one thrust of the spear. They whispered, "Seize your opportunity! Could it have fallen out more fortunately? Here is the man who has repeatedly tried to take your life, and he is here with that avowed intent. Surely the law of God itself exonerates us in taking the life of those who would take ours! God Himself has undoubtedly brought him here that you should avenge your wrongs and save further ones."

With great difficulty—and to have been able to do such a thing showed the immense power he exerted over these wild strong men—David restrained them and curbed his own passion that tore like fire through every vein. David contented himself with creeping near and cutting off the skirt of the king's robe to prove to Saul afterward how completely he had been in David's power. But even then, after Saul had left the cave and David's men crowded round, full of sullen protest at his weakness, he was struck with remorse and said to them, "The LORD forbid that I should do this thing unto my master, the LORD's anointed, to stretch forth mine hand against him, seeing he is the anointed of the LORD" (v. 6).

Hachilah. Previously at this spot, David had been nearly trapped. This time the tables were turned (1 Samuel 26). Once more, Saul, probably prompted by a malign influence, was in pursuit of his rival, "having three thousand chosen men of Israel with him" (v. 2). Having ascertained by means of scouts the exact situation of the royal camp, David went to inspect it in person from an overhanging cliff. On the outskirts, the wagons made a crude barricade, within which were the soldiers' quarters, and in the innermost circle Saul and Abner were posted. But the watches were badly kept, and no precaution was taken against a sudden attack.

A sudden inspiration seized David, and he proposed to Abishai and Ahimelech the Hittite that they should visit the camp by night. Abishai gladly volunteered to accompany him, and guided by the clear moonlight, they crept down the hill, crossed the ravine, and picked their way through the wagons and the sleeping ranks of the soldiers. Standing for a moment whispering over the prostrate form of the king, they bore off his spear and water bottle from Saul's head and then "gat them away, and no man saw it, nor knew it, neither awaked:...because a deep sleep from the LORD was fallen upon them" (1 Samuel 26:12).

Thus again Saul had been in David's power, but David had restrained himself. Abishai could not read him or understand his secret. To Abishai it seemed a most natural and lawful act for David to take the life of the man who was so infatuated for his destruction. Nay, if David were at all squeamish about killing Saul with his own hand, surely he could have no objection against Abishai's doing it, since Abishai was not personally concerned in the feud. In that whispered colloquy over the sleeping monarch, Abishai had suggested that God had delivered David's enemy into his chieftain's hand and had offered to smite Saul with his own spear with a stroke so deadly and so instantaneous that there would be neither sigh nor groan to awake Abner or his bodyguard. But David would not have it.

"No," David said. "I will be no party to this deed. None can smite the Lord's anointed and be guiltless. When his appointed death hour comes, God will take him—either by some natural process in the palace or amid the going down of the battle. But my hand shall not curtail his days. I will wait God's time."

On each of these occasions David acted with the magnanimity that became a hero and a saint. He would take no spiteful advantage of his adversary. He would not retaliate or avenge his wrong. David refused to allow the specious argument that opportunity meant permission and that license meant liberty. He quieted the impetuous fever of his soul, resisted the subtle temptation of the adversary, and elected to await the slow unfolding of the divine purpose.

THE BEHAVIOR THAT
WAITING FOR GOD INDUCES

It restrains from crime. Bitter indeed had David's remorse been had he listened to his comrades and put forth his hand against Saul's life. It would have robbed his harp of all its music. There would then have been some justification for Shimei's cursing words on that dark latter day in his life; but as it was, though the words cut him deeply, they met with no answering response from his conscience (2 Samuel 16). As David searched his heart in the sight of God, he knew that Absalom's rebellion and seizure of his throne could not be, as Shimei suggested, a requital in kind for his dealings with Saul. True, months were still to pass, full of anxiety and suspense, before the coronation shouts rang through the streets of Hebron. But the worries were forgotten as snow dissolves in the river, and then there was nothing to regret, no gnawing conscience, no emblem of death at the bottom of his cup of joy. Be still, O heart! Wait for God. This will keep you from acts and words that, if allowed, would shadow your whole afterlife.

It inspires courage. What an intrepid spirit this was that dared to cry after the king and hold up the skirt of his robe! What courage that challenged the two bravest men of his little army to a feat from which one of them shrank! Ah, the man who is living in the divine purpose has the secret of quenchless courage! He knows that no weapon formed against him shall prosper and that every tongue that shall rise against him in judgment shall be condemned. He fears nothing except to do wrong and to grieve God. If in following the prepared path he suddenly comes to the brink of a precipice, down which he must cast himself, he does not hesitate to do so. He knows that the angels will swoop beneath and bear him up so that he shall not dash his foot against a stone.

It gives great rest. Surely it was out of such experiences as these that David wrote Psalm 37, which, though it belongs to a later period, forever embalms the conclusions of this. The mellow wisdom of old age gathers up the maxims that were wrought out in the fires of early manhood:

> Fret not thyself because of evildoers,
> neither be thou envious against the workers of iniquity.
> For they shall soon be cut down like the grass,
> and wither as the green herb (v. 1–2).

The exhortations of this exquisite psalm—to trust in the Lord, to delight in the Lord, to roll the way of life on the Lord, to rest in the Lord and wait patiently for Him, and especially the repeated injunction to not fret—are all bathed in new meaning when read in the light of these memorable incidents in David's life.

Live on the divine purpose. Do not be eager for yourself, but be eager only that God's work should be done. It is certain that He will take care of your interests if you care for His. Calm yourself as a weaned child. Rest in God. Sit still and trust—God is working out the plan for your life. You cannot hurry Him. It will only expend the energy of your soul to no purpose if you allow its fever to consume you. In God's own time, the best time, He shall give you the desires of your heart.

It induces penitence in others. When David gave such unmistakable evidences of his self-restraint, continued loyalty, and surviving affection, in spite of all that had been done to quench it; when he so clearly established his innocence and showed the baselessness of the charges made against him; when he appealed with such reverence and sincerity from the calumnies and misrepresentations of earth to the decisions of the divine Judge—the miserable monarch lifted up his voice and wept, confessing that he had "played the fool, and have erred exceedingly" (1 Samuel 26:21). Saul recognized David's nobility. The old chivalrous nature that had so captivated the nation in earlier days flashed out with an expiring flicker, and he went so far as to admit that David would be king. Nothing but such forbearance on David's part could have brought him so near repentance.

It is thus that we win men still. We win most when we appear to have yielded most, and we gain advantages by refusing to take them wrongfully. The man who can wait for God is a man of power, and others will acknowledge it and bend beneath his scepter. To be under authority to God's lofty principle is to have soldiers under us who go and come at our will and do our bidding.

15

1 Samuel 26:1; Psalm 7

CUSH: A BENJAMITE

Who to that bliss aspire
Must win their way through blood and fire!—
The writhings of a wounded heart
Are fiercer than a foeman's dart.
Oft in life's stillest shade reclining,
In desolation unrepining,
Without a hope on earth to find
A mirror in an answering mind,
Meek souls these are who little deem
Their daily strife an angel's theme!

Keble

*I*t is somewhat surprising to find Saul in search of David, after the first of the incidents (1 Samuel 24) described in the previous chapter. At Engedi there seemed so absolute and entire a reconciliation between them. Saul confessed that David was more righteous than himself, acknowledged that David had dealt well with him, asked that God would reward him, and assured David that he would undoubtedly be king. He even went so far as to make David swear that when he had come to the throne he would not destroy Saul's name out of his father's house (24:21). And yet, after so short a space, he is again on the warpath.

These capricious changes may, of course, have been a result of the malady from which Saul was suffering, but another and more satisfactory explanation has been suggested, one that casts fresh light on the seventh psalm. Dr. Maclaren, whose work on the psalter has brought the whole Church into his debt, is especially emphatic in connecting Psalm 7 with this part of David's history, and he indicates its value in helping us to understand the rapid vacillations in Saul's behavior.

The psalm is headed *Shiggaion of David, which he sang unto the Lord*. This means that it is an irregular ode, like a stream broken over a bed of rocks and stones, expressing by its uneven measure and sudden changes the emotion of its author. In our lives we have often to sing these Shiggaion meters, and our songs are frequently broken with sighs and groans, but we do well still to sing with such tunefulness as we may. Happy are they who can find themes for singing to the Lord in every sad and bitter experience!

The title proceeds, *concerning the words of Cush the Benjamite*. Who was this Cush? The word means *black*. It may possibly refer to the color of the skin and hair and have been given as a familiar designation to some swarthy Benjamite with a dark complexion. Some have supposed that it was David's title for Saul, but the terms of respect in which David always spoke of the Lord's anointed make that supposition unlikely. Others have referred it to Shimei, the Benjamite, whose furious abuse of the king in the hour of David's calamity elicited such plaintive resignation from David and such passionate resentment from Abishai. But the style and phraseology belong so evidently to this period of David's life that this supposition also seems untenable.

If the psalm is carefully examined, it will be found to bear a close resemblance to the words spoken by David when Saul and he held the brief colloquy outside the cave at Engedi and afterward at the hill of Hachilah.

Indeed, the correspondences are so many and exact that they establish, almost beyond question, the date of the psalm as synchronous with the incidents described in the last chapter. And if that is the case, we can infer the cause of Saul's renewed passion. On comparison of psalm and narrative, it seems more than likely that Cush was one of Saul's intimate friends and constant companions and that he was incessantly at work poisoning the king's mind with malignant and deliberate falsehoods about David. When Saul was away from this man and under the spell of David's noble and generous nature, he laid aside his vindictiveness and responded to the appeals of olden friendship and chivalry. But when Saul returned to his palace and Cush had fresh opportunities of influencing him, Saul yielded to the worst side of his character and resumed his desperate attempt to thwart the divine purpose. Thus like a shuttlecock, he was tossed back and forth between the two men. One moment he was inclined to mercy by David, and the next to vengeance by Cush.

It is quite likely that many of those who shall read these lines will be able to understand, by bitter experiences, the anguish of David's soul from this cause. You, too, have a Cush in the circle of your life who is constantly circulating baseless and slanderous statements about you, poisoning the minds of those who otherwise would be well disposed, and suggesting questions and suspicious misunderstandings of your purest and most untainted actions. Such slanderers are to be found in every time and place, and they cause as much exquisite torture to sensitive and tender natures today as to David in the wilds of Engedi. Let us learn from David how to deal with such people.

SEARCH YOUR HEART TO SEE IF THESE SLANDERS HAVE FOUNDATION IN FACT

It may be that there is more truth in these hurtful words than you are inclined at first sight to admit. Would it not be wise to ask whether they are true before dismissing them or treating them with disdain? Perhaps those alert, envious eyes have discerned weaknesses in your character, of which your closest friends are aware but have shrunk from telling you. Remember that love is quick to notice the weak points in the beloved, though it may not always say something about them. The supreme love alone girds itself to the task of washing the feet of its friends. It is a good rule before you destroy the anonymous letter or dismiss the unkind statement to sit down before the judgment seat of Christ and in its white light ask yourself whether you can say with David: "My defence is of God, which saveth the upright in heart" (Psalm 7:10).

IF THERE IS NO BASIS FOR THEM, REJOICE!

Always remember—when men revile you and persecute you and say all manner of evil against you falsely—first, that you are in the succession of the prophets and saints of every age and may be assured that you are on the right track, and second, that out of this, according to the express words of Christ, you may extract that blessedness that is richer and deeper than the world's joy, that passes like a summer brook.

How thankful we should be that God has kept us from being actually guilty of the things whereof we are accused! We might have done them, and worse. It was only by His grace that we have been withheld. That we have the witness of a good conscience and of his Spirit in our hearts should be a perennial source of gladness.

TAKE SHELTER IN THE RIGHTEOUS JUDGMENT OF GOD

We are His servants, and if He is satisfied with us, why should we break our hearts over what others say? He put us into the positions we occupy, and if He pleases to keep us there, all that men may say or do will be unavailing to dislodge us. "It is a very small thing that I should be judged of you, or of man's judgment: yea, I judge not mine own self...but he that judgeth me is the Lord" (1 Corinthians 4:3-4). Only He can properly determine the quality of our lives, because to Him alone are the hidden things known that give the real clue to rightness or wrongness.

RENOUNCE MORE COMPLETELY THE CARNAL LIFE

Why do we hurt under these unkind and slanderous words that are as baseless as uncharitable? Is it not because we place too high a value upon the favor and applause of men? Is there not a deadly fear of being despised and condemned? Does not the world still live within us, revealing the tenacity of its hold in this mortification and shame? Is this being crucified to the world and the world crucified to us?

If we were really nothing and God were all in all; if the Spirit and the Lamb of God were dominant in our inner life; if we were dead to the flesh, with its affections and lusts, and alive only to God—surely it would be a matter of indifference what became of our good name in the lips of foolish and sinful men. Here then there is not a revelation of a deeper death to be realized. Let us not flinch from it but be willing to fall into the ground and die to our reputation, as did Jesus, who endured the opposition of sinners against

Himself and of whom they spoke as in league with Beelzebub, the prince of demons.

We must choose death in all those forms of which our Master knew it, that having been planted in the likeness of His death, we may be also in the likeness of His resurrection.

LEAVE GOD TO VINDICATE YOUR GOOD NAME

Any unjust imputation or stigma that rests on us is a manifestation of the deep-rooted evil of the world. It is a grief and care to God, and it is part of the burden that He is always carrying. It is impossible for us to cope with or remove it. It is useless to retaliate or revenge. Like Jesus, we may meekly ask the false accuser to establish his untrue charges, or we may meet them with our steadfast denial. But when we have done this, and we shall find it of little avail, there is no more to do but wait patiently till God arises to avenge our wrong and vindicate our characters.

This is the way that David acted, even in those twilight days. He appealed to the righteous God who tries the hearts of men, believing that He would gird on His armor, whet His sword, and bend His bow against those who repented not of their hatred against His saints. The psalmist had a clear apprehension of the immutable law that the wickedness of the wicked would come to an end. He believed that mischief would return on the slanderer's head, that the trapper of the saints would fall into his own snare, while the saints would be established and their character cleared. It was so that Jesus bore Himself. "Who, when he was reviled, reviled not again; when he suffered, he threatened not; but committed himself to him that judgeth righteously" (1 Peter 2:23).

Such is the true and wisest policy. Be still. Give no place to wrath. Concern yourself rather with the misery of that soul from which these wild words proceed. Think more of this than of your wrongs. Let your heart be exercised with a great tenderness towards him. If he hungers, feed him, and if he thirsts, give him drink. Try to overcome the evil of his heart by your generous good. Leave vindication and vengeance alike to God, whose prerogative is to plead the cause of the innocent and defenseless while He will repay the wrongdoer in due time.

16

1 Samuel 25

A Cool Hand On A Hot Head

Calm me, my God, and keep me calm;
Let thine outstretched wing
Be like the shade of Elim's palm,
Beside her desert spring.

Calm in the sufference of wrong,
Like Him who bore my shame;
Calm, 'mid the threatening, taunting throng,
Who hate thy holy name.

H. Bonar

*T*he tidings passed throughout the land, like fire in prairie grass, that Samuel was dead. Israel, recognizing its unity in the common loss, gathered to lament the prophet and to perform the last honoring rites. To Samuel's worth and service was accorded the unusual tribute of burial within the precincts of his own house at Ramah on the heights of Benjamin. In all likelihood, an amnesty was proclaimed, and David came to take part in the ceremonies of his master and friend. He did not, however, dare to trust himself in such near proximity to Saul a moment longer than was absolutely essential; and as soon as all was over, David started again for the sparsely populated region of Paran, at the extreme south of Judah. To those borderlands, so long desolated by border warfare through the incursions of the Philistines and Amalekites, his advent brought tranquility and safety. The sheepmasters had every reason to be grateful for his protection, and one young man said, "The men were very good unto us, and we were not hurt, neither missed we anything, as long as we were conversant with them, when we were in the fields: They were a wall unto us both by night and day, all the while we were with them keeping the sheep" (1 Samuel 25:15–16).

Where such services were accepted and counted upon, it was obviously fair—and indeed according to the custom of the time—that some type of payment should be made. It was a tacit understanding, an unwritten law. David was perfectly justified in sending ten young men to greet the wealthy sheepmaster, Nabal, in the day of prosperity—to which the exertions of himself and his men had so largely contributed—to remind him of his obligations and ask whatsoever might come readily to his hand to give. Nabal's churlish treatment of this request instantly touched David's anger and led up to an incident that, as recorded by the sacred historian, is one of the most charming idylls of Scripture, fragrant as the flowers of Alpine pastures and fresh as a summer morn. The story centers on Nabal, David, and Abigail.

NABAL, THE CHURL

Nabal's character is drawn, after the manner of Scripture, in three or four bold outline strokes and need not detain us. In every society, men of this type are to be encountered, overbearing to their inferiors, intolerable in prosperity, drunken carousers, abject in misfortune. There are always those who fly out with contempt and sneer when they think themselves secure but whose heart cringes before reverse. What an apt thumbnail sketch is given of the whole race of Nabals in the confidential remark passed between his servant and his wife: "He is such a son of Belial, that a man cannot speak to him" (1 Samuel 25:17)!

He was very great, the historian says. But it was the poorest kind of greatness, consisting not in what he was in character or had achieved in valiant deed but in the number of sheep and goats that bore his brand over the pasturelands of the south. There are four kinds of greatness, so be wise and choose the best for your life aim! It is a small thing to possess many things, better to be great in doing, better still to conceive and proclaim great thoughts, but best to be great in character. Aim at the greatness of which heaven takes account. It was where self-mastery, Holy Ghost fullness, and service to mankind met that the angel said, "He shall be great in the sight of the Lord" (Luke 1:15).

He was a fool, Abigail said. "For as his name is, so is he; Nabal is his name, and folly is with him" (1 Samuel 25:25). Poor woman! She had every reason for speaking so bitterly of him; and she was a sweet woman, too, not likely to speak in these terms of her husband unless his rude, cruel hands had wantonly broken down the last remnant of her respect and love. He surely must have sat for the full-length portrait of the fool in our Lord's parable, who thought his soul could take its ease and be merry because a few big barns were full. There are appetites and longings in the soul that good dinners cannot satisfy. There are cravings that will not be appeased merely because we can see our way to three meals a day as long as we live.

He was a man of Belial, his servant said. And indeed his treatment of David's modest request well bore out the character. It was rude, discourteous, uncivil. He could not have been ignorant of the causes that had forced David into his wandering, arduous life, but he ignored them and chose to put forward the most cruel and harsh construction. He could have as easily said that David was raising a revolt against his master Saul and virtuously covered his refusal beneath a show of loyal devotion to law and government, which was intended to suggest an extremely unpleasant alternative for David. Nabal asserted his preference to give his food to those who, like his shearers, had worked for it, rather than to a lot of vain fellows who were hanging idly about to live on the ripe fruit that might fall into their mouths.

He seems to have had no prick of conscience for his churlish speeches and no idea of the consequences they might involve. As soon as the words were spoken, they were forgotten. In the evening of the day on which they were spoken, we find Nabal in his house, holding a feast, like the feast of a king, his heart merry with wine, and altogether so stupid that his wife told him nothing till the morning light.

DAVID, HASTY AND PASSIONATE

One of the most characteristic features in David's temper and behavior through all these weary years was his self-control. He waited patiently for the Lord. Year after year he stayed himself on

God's promise and left Him to fulfill the word on which He had caused David to hope. When summoned to relieve Ziklag or warned to leave it, as well as on other occasions, he showed the utmost deliberation, calling for prophet or priest and seeking to ascertain the divine will before taking a step. On two occasions, David had controlled himself, when Saul lay in his power, and refused to take Saul's life. But the rampart of self-restraint built by long habit went down like a neglected sea wall before the sudden paroxysm of passion that Nabal's insulting words aroused. In hot fury, he said to his men, "Gird ye on every man his sword. And they girded on every man his sword; and David also girded on his sword: and there went up after David about four hundred men" (1 Samuel 25.13). He undoubtedly argued with himself as they marched rapidly through the silent fields: "I am justified in this act. There is no reason why this man should treat me like this. He has returned evil for good and added reviling and reproach. It is intolerable. I must assert my self-respect and let this neighborhood see that I am not going to take it. I will bear from the king what I will suffer from no other living man."

At this hour, David was on the brink of committing a crime that would have cast a dark shadow on all his latter years. In calmer, quieter, holier hours, it would have been a grief to him and an offense of heart to have shed blood causelessly and avenged himself instead of leaving it to the Lord. From this shame, sorrow, and disgrace, he was saved by that sweet and noble woman, Abigail.

ABIGAIL, THE BEAUTIFUL INTERCESSOR

Abigail was a woman of good understanding and of a beautiful countenance. Her character had written its legend on her face. The two things do not always go together. There are many beautiful women wholly destitute of good understanding. But a good understanding, which is moral rather than intellectual, casts a glow of beauty over the commonest features.

It is remarkable how many Abigails get married to Nabals. God-fearing women, tender and gentle in their sensibilities, high-minded and noble in their ideals, become tied to an indissoluble union with men for whom they can have no true affinity, even if they have not an unconquerable abhorrence. In Abigail's case, this relationship was in all probability not of her choosing but was the product of the

Eastern custom that compelled a girl to take her father's choice in the matter of marriage. As a mere child, Abigail may have come into Nabal's home and become bound to him by an apparently inevitable fate. In other ways, whether compelled by the pressure of inexorable circumstances, misled by the deceitful tongue of flattery, her instinctive hesitance overcome by the urgency of friends, a woman may still find herself in Abigail's pitiful plight. To such a woman, there is but one advice—you must stay where you are. The dissimilarity in taste and temperament does not constitute a sufficient reason for leaving your husband to drift. You must believe that God has permitted you to enter on this awful heritage, partly because this fiery ordeal was required by your character and partly that you might act as a counteractive influence. You must stay as you are. It may be that someday your opportunity will come, as it came to Abigail. In the meantime, do not allow your purer nature to be tainted. You can always keep the soul clean and pure. Bide your time, and amid the weltering waste of inky water be like a pure fountain rising from the ocean depths.

But if any woman of good sense and earnest aspirations who reads these lines secretly knows that if she had the chance she would marry into a good position and wealth, irrespective of character, let her remember that to enter the marriage bond with a man for such a purpose is a profanation of the divine ideal and can end only in one way. She will not raise him to her level but will sink to his; her marble will not change his clay but will coarsen to it.

Nabal's servants knew the quality of their mistress and could trust her to act wisely in the emergency that was upon them, so they told her all. She immediately grasped the situation, dispatched a small procession of provision bearers along the way that David must come, and followed them immediately. She met the avenging warriors by the covering of the mountain, and the interview was as creditable to her woman's wit as to her grace of heart. The lowly obeisance of the beautiful woman at the soldier's feet, the frank confession of the wrong that had been done, the expression of thankfulness that so far David had been kept from bloodguiltiness and from avenging his own wrongs, the depreciation of the generous present she brought as only fit for David's servants, the chivalrous appreciation of David's desire to fight only the battles of the Lord and to keep an unblemished name, the sure anticipation of the time when his fortunes would be secured and his enemies silenced, the suggestion that in those coming days David would be glad to have no shadow on the sunlit hills of his life, no haunting memory—all this was as beautiful and wise and womanly as it could be, and it brought David back to his better self. Frank and noble as he always was, David did not hesitate to acknowledge his deep indebtedness to this lovely woman and to see in her intercession the gracious arrest of God. "And David said to Abigail, Blessed be the Lord God of Israel, which sent thee this day to meet me: And blessed be thy advice, and blessed be thou, which hast kept me this day from coming to shed blood, and from avenging myself with mine own hand" (1 Samuel 25:32–33).

What a revelation this is of the ministries with which God seeks to avert us from our evil ways! They are sometimes very subtle and tender, very small and still. Sometimes a gentle woman's hand laid on our wrist, the mother reminding us of her care, the wife of early vows, the child with his pitiful beseeching look; sometimes a thought—holy, pleading, remonstrating. Ah, many a time we have been saved from actions that would have caused lasting regret had we not heeded! And above all these voices and influence, there has been the gracious arresting influences of the Holy Spirit, striving with passion and selfishness, calling us to a nobler life. Blessed Spirit, come down more often as Abigail did and keep us from our own destruction. Let us not press past You to take our own wild way, and we shall have reason for ceaseless gratitude.

The idyll ended happily. Nabal died in a sudden stroke caused by his debauchery or his anger at his wife's treatment of David and his men. And David made proposals of marriage to the woman to whom he owed so much, which she gracefully and humbly accepted, not thinking herself worthy for such high honor. "Behold," she said, "let thine handmaid be a servant to wash the feet of the servants of my lord" (1 Samuel 25:41). I suppose that in this life or the next, all God's idylls end happily. That, at least, is one cherished article of my creed.

17

1 Samuel 27

A FIT
OF MISTRUST

Ever thus the spirit must,
Guilty in the sight of heaven,
With a keener woe be riven,
For its weak and sinful trust
In the strength of human dust;
And its anguish thrill afresh
For each vain reliance given
To the failing arm of flesh.

Whittier

*T*he psalms that with a good probability may be assigned to this period of David's life are marked with growing sadness and depression. Among them may be considered Psalms 10, 13, 17, 22, 23, 64, and perhaps 40 and 69. Those of the first group have many features in common. The scenery of the wilderness, the psalmist like a hunted wild thing, the perpetual insistence on his innocence and invocation of Jehovah's interference, the bitter description of his sorrows—such are the characteristic features of these psalms. But, besides, there is a tone of despair:

Why standest thou afar off, O LORD?
why hidest thou thyself in times of trouble? (10:1)

111

How long wilt thou forget me, O LORD? for ever?
how long wilt thou hide thy face from me? (13:1)

My God, my God, why hast thou forsaken me?
why art thou so far from helping me, and from the words of
my roaring? (22:1)

Save me, O God; for the waters are come in unto my soul.
I sink in deep mire, where there is no standing:
I am come into deep waters, where the floods overflow me
(69:1–2).

These notes are sad, plaintive, and despairful. It is as though
the sufferer were near the limits of his endurance. It seemed hopeless to effect any permanent alteration in Saul's feelings toward
David, as long as Cush and Doeg and Abner and others who had
proved themselves his inveterate foes yet able to so readily instill
their poison into the royal ear. It had become so increasingly difficult to elude the hot pursuit of the royal troops, whom long practice
had familiarized with David's hiding places and haunts. And it
became more and more perplexing to find sustenance for the large
body of followers now attached to him. Every day David had to provide for six hundred men, besides women and children. And the
presence of these more tender souls made it perilously difficult to
maintain a perpetual condition of migration or flight. David now
had two wives; and from what is said of the latter pillaging of
Ziklag, we should judge that the larger proportion of the outlawed
band consisted of those who had wives and sons and daughters and
property (1 Samuel 30: 3, 6, 19, 22).

In other days of healthier faith, these considerations would not
have prevailed to shake the constancy of David's much-tried soul.
David would have stayed himself upon his God and been strengthened with all power, unto all patience and longsuffering with joy.
But of late his faith had become impaired and the strength of his
godly courage slackened so that he said in his heart, "I shall now
perish one day by the hand of Saul: there is nothing better for me
than that I should speedily escape into the land of the Philistines;
and Saul shall despair of me, to seek me any more in any coast of
Israel: so shall I escape out of his hand" (1 Samuel 27:1).

LET US EXAMINE THIS SUDDEN RESOLUTION

It was the suggestion of worldly policy. "David said in his heart."
On other occasions, as we have observed more than once, it had
been his custom to summon the priest with the sacred ephod or to
inquire of God through Gad. But in this resolution, David had
recourse to neither the one nor the other. In the matter of Nabal, he
had acted under the sudden pulse of passion; here he is acting
under that of panic. He looked at circumstances and perhaps listened to the counsel of men who were attracted to him by the qualities of daring, bravery, and frank generosity but who had no sympathy with the deeper springs of his life in God and faith and prayer.
Never act in a panic. Never allow a man to dictate to you. Calm
yourself and be still. Force yourself into the quiet of your closet until
the pulse beats normally and the scare has ceased to perturb. When
you are most eager to act is the time when you will make the most
pitiable mistakes. Do not say in your heart what you will or will not
do, but wait upon God until He makes known His way. So long as
that way is hidden, it is clear that there is no need of action and that
God accounts Himself responsible for all the results of keeping you
where you are.

It was very dishonoring to God. Had He not sworn to make
David king, to cast forth his enemies as out of a sling, and to give
him a sure house? Had not these promises been confirmed by
Samuel, Jonathan, Abigail, and Saul himself? Had not the golden oil
designated him as God's anointed? How impossible it was that God
should lie or forget His covenant! By immutable pledges David's
Almighty Friend had bound Himself, seeking to give His much-tried
child strong encouragement, if only David would remain within the
sheltering walls of the refuge harbor that these assurances constituted. And it was easier for heaven and earth to pass away than for
one jot or tittle of the divine promises to become invalid.

Surely, then, it was unworthy of David to say, in effect: "I am
beginning to fear that God has undertaken more than He can carry
through. True, He has kept me so far, but I question whether He can
help me overcome the growing difficulties of my situation. Saul will,
sooner or later, accomplish his designs against me. It is a mistake to
attempt the impossible. I have waited till I am tired. Now it is time
to use my own wits and extricate myself while I can from the nets
that are being drawn over my path."

The resolution must have given great rejoicing to many of David's followers. But all devout souls must have felt that the leader's despairing confession was in sad contrast to his exhortation—so repeatedly insisted upon—to wait on God.

How much easier it is to indicate a true course to others in hours of comparative security than to stand to it under a squall of wind! Dr. Tauler, the great preacher of Strasburg, before his second and deeper conversion, could be excelled by none in his outlining of the virtues of humility and self-denial. Yet, when it was brought to his attention that he loved one creature—himself—more than God, Tauler was offended and his proud heart arose within him. It is an experience through which most of us have to pass—the contrast between speech and possession, between thinking we have and having, between our directions to others and our own behavior when the dark waters are sweeping over our soul.

It was highly injurious. Philistia was full of idol temples and idolatrous priests (2 Samuel 5:21). It lay outside the inheritance of the Lord, the sacred land of Palestine, deemed by the pious Israelites of those days to be the special location and abiding place of the Most High. To be banished from those sacred borders seemed like going into a wild and desolate land of estrangement and God abandonment. What fellowship could David look for with the divine Spirit who had chosen Israel for His people and Jacob for the lot of His inheritance? How could he sing the Lord's songs in a strange land? What share could he claim in the sacrifices that sent up the thin spiral of smoke on the sites of Nob or Kirjath-Jearim? Besides, their perpetual familiarity with the rites and iniquities of idolatry could not but exert an unwholesome and altogether disastrous effect on the minds of the unstable in his band. Poison must have been injected into many hearts that wrought disastrously in later years. What was harmless enough in the case of David, who knew that an idol was nothing in the world, was perilous in the extreme to the weak consciences to some of his men who were defiled by what they saw and heard.

It was the entrance on a course that demanded the perpetual practice of deceit. David was received at Gath with open arms. Before, when he had sought the shelter of the court of Achish, he had but a handful of companions. Now he was the leader of a formidable band of warriors, who might easily turn the scale of strength in the long struggle between Israel and Philistia. "And David dwelt with Achish at Gath, he and his men, every man with his household" (1 Samuel 27:3).

This proximity to the royal palace and the court became, however, extremely irksome to the Hebrews. Their movements were always under inspection, and it was difficult to preserve their autonomy and independence. Finally, therefore, David asked that one of the smaller towns might be assigned to him. To his great comfort, they received permission to settle at Ziklag, a town in the south country, originally allotted to Judah, then transferred to Simeon, and later captured by the Philistines but not occupied by them (Joshua 15:31; 19:5; 1 Chronicles 4:30).

The sense of security and relief to these hunted men must have been very great, as they found themselves within the slender fortifications of the little town. For so long they had known no settled home, their life full of alarm and flight, the weapon always at their side or in their hand, the senses alert to the rustle of a leaf or the slightest movement in the covert; from all these there was now a grateful pause. For sixteen months they had a measure of repose and safety. The old men and women sat in the streets, and the shouts of merry children in their play were no longer instantly and jealously hushed lest they should attract the scouts of the royal army. "And it was told Saul that David was fled to Gath: and he sought no more again for him" (1 Samuel 27:4).

David's mind was, however, kept on the stretch, constantly at work, weaving a fabric of duplicity and cruelty. David had really no love for Achish or zeal for the maintenance of Achish's rule. David had not deserted the chosen people, though he had fled before Saul. In his deepest soul, David was still a Hebrew of the Hebrews. Provisions for himself and his followers must, of course, be provided, and in those days of wild border-war, nothing was more obvious—to the Philistines, at least—than to raid the land on which David had turned his back. This, of course, David would not do, and so he turned his sword on the petty tribes of the south country who were in alliance with the Philistines but the hereditary foes of his own people. Among them were the Geshurites, the Girzites, and the Amalekites—all nomad tribes who lived by plunder. To prevent any report of his proceedings reaching the ears of Achish, David was compelled to adopt the cruel and murderous policy of saving neither man nor woman alive. When Achish, by virtue of his feudal lordship, required of David an account of his expedition, David said evasively that he had been raiding against the south of Judah and cited tribes that were known to be under the direct protection of Israel. The fact of his having brought back no captives, the most valuable part of booty, was reckoned by the Philistines a proof of the passionate hate with which David regarded his countrymen, making him forgo the financial advantage accruing from the sale of slaves rather than the satisfaction of beholding their dying anguish. "And Achish believed David, saying, He hath made his people Israel utterly to abhor him; therefore he shall be my servant for ever" (1 Samuel 27:12).

The whole behavior of David at this time was utterly unworthy of his high character as God's anointed servant. *It was also a barren time in his religious experience.* No psalms are credited to this period. The sweet singer was mute. He probably acquired a few new strains of music or even mastered some fresh instruments while sojourning at Gath, the memory of which is perpetuated in the term *Gittith*, which frequently occurs in the inscriptions of the psalms composed afterward. But who would trade a song for a melody, a psalm for a guitar? It was a poor exchange. There was something in the air of those lowland plains that closed the utterances of the sweet voice that had sung to God amid the hills of Judah and the caves of Ain-jedi.

How precisely do these symptoms of decline and relapse correspond with those that we have observed in ourselves and others! The way of faith may be irksome to the flesh, but it is free and glad to the spirit. It may have to trace its steps with difficulty among the hills, but a new song of praise and thanksgiving is in its mouth. But when we descend to the lowlands of expediency and worldly policy, a blight comes on the landscape of the soul, a silence on the song of the heart.

From the moment we are left to maintain our position by our own scheming and planning, we ask God to help us but dare not count on Him absolutely to provide for us. We are driven into tight corners, from which we escape by deception and duplicity, such as we in our souls despise. We realize that we have purchased our deliverance from the pressure of adverse circumstances at too great a cost and have exchanged the smile of God for that of Achish, so soon to be turned from us. We have traded the munitions of divine protection for the walls of Ziklag, over the ruins of which we shall soon be weeping scalding tears.

18

1 Samuel 29, 30

THE MERCY
OF GOD THAT
LED TO REPENTANCE

Prostrate your soul in penitential prayer!
Humble your heart beneath the mighty hand
Of God, Whose gracious guidance oft shall lead
Through sin and crime the changed and melted heart,
To sweet repentance and the sense of Him.

Clough

*T*hroughout the season of declension and relapse that we have been considering, the loving mercy of God hovered tenderly over David's life. "If we believe not, yet he abideth faithful: he cannot deny himself" (2 Timothy 2:13). When God's servants are wandering far afield, sowing for themselves thistledown and piercing themselves through with bitter sorrows, He is encompassing their path and their lying down, solicitous of heart and compassionate, exhibiting the tenderest traits of His mercy and pity, as though to win them back to Himself.

This is particularly illustrated by the present stage of David's history. There was a special focusing of divine gentleness and goodness to withdraw him from his purpose, to keep back his soul from the pit and his life from perishing with the sword. We will now trace the successive stages in this loving process of divine restoration, and as we do so, we will believe that in all these things God still works to bring back our souls from the pit, that we may be enlightened with the light of life. In us also, David's word shall be verified, spoken as he reviewed this part of his career from the pinnacle of prosperity and glory to which God's goodness afterwards raised him: "Thy gentleness hath made me great" (Psalm 18:35). God's restoring mercy was evident in the following ways.

IN INCLINING STRONG AND NOBLE MEN TO IDENTIFY WITH DAVID'S CAUSE

"Now these are they," says the chronicler, "that came to David to Ziklag, while he yet kept himself close because of Saul the son of Kish: and they were among the mighty men, helpers of the war" (1 Chronicles 12:1). And he proceeds to enumerate them. Some came from Saul's own tribe, experienced marksmen, who could use with equal dexterity the right hand and the left, in slinging stones and in shooting arrows from the bow. Some came from the eastern bank of the Jordan, swimming it at the flood; mighty men of valor, men trained for war, whose faces were like the faces of lions, and they were as swift as deer among the mountains. Some came from Benjamin and Judah, assuring David that there was no ground for his suspicions of their loyalty. What a manly, generous ring there was in those reassuring words as uttered by their leader, Amasai, and which were probably the expression of the feelings of all the contingents of heroes who at this time rallied around David's standard: "Thine are we, David, and on thy side, thou son of Jesse: peace, peace be unto thee, and peace be to thine helpers; for thy God helpeth thee" (1 Chronicles 12:18).

Evidently the spirit of discontent was abroad in the land. The people, weary of Saul's oppression and misgovernment, were beginning to realize that the true hope of Israel lay in the son of Jesse. They therefore went out to David without the camp, bearing his reproach, content to forfeit everything they possessed in the assurance that they would receive it all again, and a hundredfold beside, when he came by his own. Thus from day to day "there came to David to help him, until it was a great host, like the host of God" (1 Chronicles 12:22).

118

Similarly, in silence and secrecy, loyal and true hearts are gathering around our blessed Lord, the center of whose Kingdom is not earthly but heavenly. Jesus Christ has gone away to receive a Kingdom, but He shall certainly return. And when He is manifested in His kingly glory, then His saints shall also be manifested with Him. Who then are willing to leave the tottering realm of the prince of this world, soon to be shattered on the last great battlefield of time, and identify themselves with the Kingdom of the Son of David, which is destined to endure as long as the sun?

IN FREEING HIS SERVANT FROM THE FALSE POSITION INTO WHICH HE HAD DRIFTED

The Philistines suddenly resolved on an aggressive policy. They were aware of the disintegration that was slowly dividing Saul's kingdom, and they had noticed with secret satisfaction the growing numbers of mighty men who were leaving it to seek identification with David and therefore, presumably, with themselves. Not content with the border hostilities that had engaged them so long, they resolved to follow the course of the maritime plain—the long stretch of low-lying land on the shores of the Mediterranean—and to strike a blow in the very heart of the land, the fertile plain of Esdraelon, destined to be one of the greatest battlefields of the world. It would one day be drenched with the blood of great leaders, as Sisera, Saul, and Joash, and of vast hosts, Philistine and Hebrew, Egyptian and Assyrian, Roman and Maccabean, Saracen and Anglo-Saxon. "Now the Philistines gathered together all their armies to Aphek: and the Israelites pitched by a fountain which is in Jezreel" (1 Samuel 29:1).

When this campaign was being planned, the guileless king assured David that he should accompany him. This was perhaps said as a mark of special confidence. It would have been foolhardy on the part of Achish to associate David with himself on such an expedition had he not conceived the most absolute confidence in David's integrity. Achish had seen no fault in his *protege* from the first hour of David's coming into his court but had looked on him as an angel of God. Achish had no hesitation, therefore, in summoning David to march beside him and even to be captain of his bodyguard. "Therefore will I make thee keeper of mine head for ever" (1 Samuel 28:2). It was a relief to the gentle nature of the king to turn from his imperious lords to this generous, open-hearted soul and entrust himself to David's strong care.

It was, however, a very critical juncture with David. He had no alternative but to follow his liege lord into the battle, but it must have been with a sinking heart. It looked as though David would be forced to fight Saul, from whom for so many years he had fled. And to fight against Saul included Jonathan, his beloved friend, and the chosen people, over whom he hoped one day to rule. David could only reply evasively and with a forced composure: "Surely thou shalt know what thy servant can do"(1 Samuel 28:2). But every mile of those fifty or sixty that had to be traversed must have been trodden with a sullen face and troubled heart. There was no hope for him in man. It may be; that already David's heart was turning in eager prayer to God, that He would help David escape the net that his sins had woven for his feet. In the evasiveness of the reply David gave to Achish is a trace of glimmering hope that God would yet extricate him from his fearful dilemma.

If by your mistakes and sins you have reduced yourself to a compromising position like this, do not despair. Hope still in God. Confess and put away your sin and humble yourself before God, and He will arise to deliver you. You may have destroyed yourself, but in Jesus Christ will be your help. "But if ye turn unto me, and keep my commandments, and do them; though there were of you cast out unto the uttermost part of the heaven, yet will I gather them from thence, and will bring them unto the place that I have chosen to set my name there" (Nehemiah 1:9).

An unexpected door of hope was suddenly opened in this valley of Achor. When Achish reviewed his troops in Aphek, after the lords of the Philistines had passed on by hundreds and by thousands, David and his men passed on toward the rear with the king. This aroused the jealousy and suspicion of the imperious Philistine princes, and they came to Achish with fierce words and threats. "What do these Hebrews here?... Make this fellow return, that he may go again to his place which thou hast appointed him, and let him not go down with us to battle" (1 Samuel 29:3-4). In vain Achish pleaded on the behalf of David, but the Philistines would have none of it. They pointed out how virulent a foe David had been and how tempting an opportunity it was for him to purchase reconciliation with Saul by turning traitor in the fight. In the end, therefore, the king had to yield. It cost him much to inform David of the inevitable decision to which he was driven, but little did he realize what a burst of relief his announcement would give. We can imagine David saying to himself as he left the royal pavilion: "Our soul is escaped as a bird out of the snare of the fowlers: the snare is broken, and we are escaped" (Psalm 124:7).

David did make a show of injured innocence: "But what have I done? and what hast thou found in thy servant so long as I have been with thee unto this day, that I may not go fight against the enemies of my lord the king?" (1 Samuel 29:8). But David's heart was not with his words, and it was with unfeigned satisfaction that he received the stringent command to depart from the camp with the morning light. As in the gray dawn David stealthily mustered his men to start, did he not fling one glance as far as the mists permitted to the camp of Israel, where the lionheart of the beloved Jonathan was doubtless preparing himself for the fight? How David must have desired to have been permitted to be beside Jonathan in repelling one of the most formidable invasions of their lives!

BY THE DIVINE DEALINGS WITH DAVID WITH RESPECT TO THE BURNING OF ZIKLAG

It was by God's great mercy that the Philistine lords were so set against David continuing in their camp. They thought that they were executing a piece of ordinary policy, dictated by prudence and foresight, little realizing that they were the shears by which God was cutting the meshes of David's net. Their protest was lodged at exactly the right moment. Had it been postponed but for a few hours, David would have been involved in the battle and would not have been back in time to overtake the Amalekites red-handed in the sack of Ziklag .

As David was leaving the battlefield, a number of the men of Manasseh, who appear to have deserted to Achish, were assigned to him by the Philistines lest they also should turn traitors on the field. Thus David left the camp with a greatly increased following. Here, too, was a proof of God's tender thoughtfulness, because at no time of his life was David in greater need of reinforcements than now. God anticipates coming trials and reinforces us against their certain imminence and pressure. We are taken into the House Beautiful to be armed before we descend into the valley of conflict with Apollyon.

It was altogether according to God's merciful providence that contrary to his custom David had left no men to defend Ziklag during his absence. It is difficult to understand the laxity of his arrangements for its safety in those wild and perilous times, but apparently no soldiers were left to protect the women and children. Yet it worked out for good, because when a band of Amalekites fell suddenly on the little town there was none to irritate them by offering resistance, no one to obstruct their will, nothing to excite their fear of pursuit or revenge. It appeared that neither David nor his soldiers would be back from the war for weeks or months. So the Amalekites felt they had no need to exercise the usual precautions—and could eat and drink and feast.

In the first outburst of grief and horror, nothing but the gracious interposition of God could have saved David's life. On reaching the spot that they called home, after three days' exhausting march, the soldiers found it a heap of smoldering ruins. Instead of the welcome of wives and children, silence and desolation reigned supreme. "Then David and the people that were with him lifted up their voice and wept, until they had no more power to weep" (1 Samuel 30:4). But in David's case there was an added element of distress. Those who had a little before cried, "Peace, peace to thee, thou son of Jesse, for thy God helpeth thee" (1 Chronicles 12:18), now spoke of stoning him. The loyalty and devotion that David had never failed to receive from his followers were suddenly changed to vinegar and gall. The milk of human kindness had turned sour in this awful thunderstorm.

But this was the moment of David's return to God. In that dread hour, with the charred embers smoking at his feet, with the cold hand of anxiety for the fate of his wives tearing his heart, with the sense of duplicity and deceit that he had been practicing and had alienated him from God, with the threat of stoning in his ears, David's heart suddenly sprang back into its old resting place in the bosom of God. "And David was greatly distressed; for the people spake of stoning him, because the soul of all the people was grieved, every man for his sons and for his daughters: *but David encouraged himself in the Lord his God* (1 Samuel 30:6).

From this moment David is himself again, his strong, glad, noble self. For the first time, after months of disuse, he bids Abiathar bring him the ephod, and he inquires of the Lord. With marvelous vigor he arises to pursue the marauding troop, and he overtakes it. He withholds the impulsiveness of his men till daylight wanes, loosing them from the leash in the twilight and leading them to the work of rescue and vengeance with such driving force that not a man of them escaped, save four hundred young men who rode upon camels and fled. And when the greed of David's followers proposed to withhold all share in the rich plunder from those whose faintness had kept them by the brook Besor, David dared to stand alone against the whole of them. He insisted that it should not be so but that their shares should be equal. Thus he who had power with God had power also with man.

And when, shortly after, the breathless messenger burst into David's presence with the tidings of Gilboa's fatal rout, though the news meant the fulfillment of David's long-delayed hopes, David was able to bear himself humbly and with unaffected sorrow, to express his lament in the most exquisite funeral ode in existence, and to award the Amalekite his punishment.

David was sweet as well as strong, as courteous as brave. For when he returned to Ziklag, his first act was to send of the spoil taken from the Amalekites to the elders of all the towns on the southern frontier where he and his men had customarily hidden from Saul, acknowledging his indebtedness to them, and so far as possible requiting it.

Thus the sunshine of God's favor rested afresh upon his soul. David had broken from Doubting Castle and Giant Despair and had reached again the path of obedience and safety. God had brought him up from the horrible pit and the miry clay, setting his feet upon a rock and putting a new song of praise in his mouth. Let all backsliders give heed and take comfort. These things were written for our instruction, that we, through the comfort and instruction of the Scriptures, might have hope.

19

2 Samuel 1–4

THRICE CROWNED

For life, with all it yields of joy and woe,
Is just our chance o' the prize of learning love;
And that we hold henceforth to the uttermost
Such prize, dispite the envy of the world.

R. Browning

*T*wo whole days had passed since that triumphant march back from the slaughter of Amalek to the charred and blackened ruins of Ziklag, and it appeared that David was waiting for some sign to determine his future course. What should he do next? Should he begin to build again the ruined city? Or was there something else in the divine program of his life? His heart was on the lookout. David could not forget that when, but a few days back, he had left the camp of Achish, a battle was imminent between the Philistines and his countrymen. Had that battle been fought? And if so, what had happened? What tidings were there of Saul, of the beloved Jonathan, and of his comrades? Surely it could not be long before rumors, breathed as on the wind, would answer the questions that were surging through his mind.

On the third day a young man rushed breathless into the camp, his clothes torn and earth upon his head. He made straight for David and fell to the ground at David's feet. In a moment more, his tidings were told, each word stabbing David to the heart. Israel had fled before the foe; large numbers were fallen on the battlefield; Saul and Jonathan were dead also. In that moment, David knew that the thundercloud that had been so long hanging over his head had broken and that the expectations of years were on the point of being realized. But David had no thought for himself or for the marvelous change in his fortunes. His generous soul, oblivious to itself, poured out a flood of the noblest tears man ever shed, for Saul and for Jonathan his son and for the people of the Lord and for the house of Israel because they were fallen by the sword.

DAVID'S TREATMENT OF SAUL'S MEMORY

There could be no doubt that Saul was dead. His crown, the symbol of kingly power, and the bracelet worn upon his arm were already in David's possession. The Amalekite indeed, to put David more absolutely under obligation, had made it appear that the king's life had been taken, at Saul's own request, by himself. "He said unto me again," so the man's tale ran, "'Stand, I pray thee, upon me, and slay me: for anguish is come upon me, because my life is yet whole in me.' So I stood upon him, and slew him, because I was sure that he could not live after that he was fallen" (2 Samuel 1:9–10). David seems to have been as one stunned till the evening, and then he aroused himself to show respect to Saul's memory.

He gave the Amalekite his due reward. The bearer of the sad news had been held under arrest because on his own showing he had slain the Lord's anointed. And as the evening fell, the wretched man was again brought into the chieftain's presence. David seems to have had some doubt as to his tale, and it afterward appeared that the story was false. Still it was necessary that the regicide should pay the extreme penalty for the deed that he had confessed.

With the reverence for the Lord's anointing that had smitten him to the heart when he cut off the piece of his robe, David asked, an expression of horror in his tone, "How wast thou not afraid to stretch forth thine hand to destroy the LORD's anointed?" (2 Samuel 1:14). Then calling one of his young men, David commanded him, "Go near, and fall upon him. And he smote him that he died" (2 Samuel 1:15).

He next poured out his grief in The Song of the Bow, which at first was taught to and sung by the children of Judah and has since passed into the literature of the world as an unrivaled model of a funeral dirge. The Dead March in *Saul* is a familiar strain in every national mourning. It was originally called the Song of the Bow (2 Samuel 1:18, R.V.), because of the reference to that weapon in the poem.

The greatness of Israel's loss is brought out in the fancied exaltation with which the daughters of Philistia would welcome their returning warriors, in the lasting curse invoked on the mountains where the shield of the mighty was polluted with gore and dust, and in the exploits that the heroes wrought with bow and sword before they fell. And then the psalmist bursts into heart-rending reminiscences of the ancient friendship that had bound him to the departed. David forgets all he had suffered at the hands of Saul and thinks only of the ideal of his early manhood. His chivalrous love refuses to consider anything but what had been brave and fair and noble in his liege lord before self-will had dragged down Saul's soul into the murky abyss, where for the last few years it had been entombed as in a living grave. "Lovely and pleasant," such is the epitaph he inscribes on the memorial stone (2 Samuel 1:23).

But for Jonathan there must be a special stanza. Might had been his, as Saul's. Had he not attacked an army single-handed and wrought a great deliverance? But with all his strength, he had been sweet. A brother-soul, every memory of whom was very pleasant, like a sweet strain of music or the scent of the spring breeze. Tender, gentle, loving as a woman. A knightly nature, dreaded by foe, dearly loved by friend, terrible as a whirlwind in battle but capable of exerting all the fascination of a woman's love, and more: "Thy love to me was wonderful, passing the love of women" (2 Samuel 1:26).

Moreover, he sent a message of thanks and congratulation to the men of Jabesh-gilead. The indignity with which the Philistines had treated the royal bodies had been amply atoned for by the devotion of the men of Jabesh-gilead. They had not forgotten that Saul's first act as king had been to deliver them from a horrible fate, so they had organized an expedition that had taken the bodies of Saul and his three sons from the walls of Bethshan, to which, after being beheaded, they were affixed. The men had carried the bodies through the night to their own city, where they had burned them to save them from further dishonor—the ashes being reverently buried under the tamarisk tree in Gilead.

As soon as David heard of this act, he sent messengers to the men of Jabesh-gilead, thanking them for their chivalrous devotion to the memory of the fallen king and promising to requite the kindness as a deed done to the entire nation and to himself.

In all this David showed great magnanimity. There was no thought of himself or his own interests. He had learned the secret of escaping from himself in his devotion and care for another. It is the secret of all self-forgetfulness. Live in another's life, especially in the interests of your Master, Jesus Christ, and you will be freed from the constant obtrusion and tyranny of self.

DAVID'S ATTITUDE WITH RESPECT TO THE KINGDOM

There is something very beautiful in David's movements at this juncture, evidencing how completely his soul had come back to its resting in God. He had resumed his old attitude of waiting only upon God and directing all his expectation to Him. It was for God to give him the kingdom, and therefore David refused to take one step toward the throne apart from the direct divine impulse.

This was the most remarkable, when so many reasons might have been alleged for immediate action. The kingdom was overrun by Philistines. Indeed, it is probable that for the next five years there was no settled government among the northern tribes. It must have been difficult for his patriot heart to restrain itself from gathering the scattered forces of Israel and flinging himself on the foe. David knew, too, that he was God's designated king, and it would have been only natural for him immediately to step up to the empty throne, assuming the scepter as his right. Possibly none would have disputed a vigorous, decisive policy of this sort. Abner might have been outmaneuvered and have shrunk from setting up Ish-bosheth at Mahanaim. So mere human judgment might have reasoned. But David was better advised. Refusing to judge according to the judgment of his eyes, he inquired of the Lord, saying, "Shall I go up into any of the cities of Judah?" (2 Samuel 2:1). And when the divine oracle directed him to proceed to Hebron, David does not appear to have gone there in any sense as king or leader but settled quietly with his followers among the towns and villages in its vicinity, waiting until the men of Judah came and by a consentaneous movement owned him king. Then for a second time he was anointed.

Anointed first by Samuel in the secrecy of his father's house, David was now anointed king over his own people. Similarly, as the Lord Jesus, of whom David was the great exemplar and type, was anointed first by the banks of the Jordan and then a second time as the representative of His people when He ascended for them into the presence of the Father and was set as King on the holy hill of Zion.

We cannot turn from David's second anointing without emphasizing the obvious lesson that at each great crisis of our life, and especially when standing on the threshold of some new and enlarged sphere of service, we should seek and receive a fresh anointing to equip us to fulfill its fresh demands. There should be successive and repeated anointings in our life history as our opportunities widen out in ever-increasing circles. It is a mistake to be always looking back to an anointing we have received: we must be anointed with fresh oil. When leaving for college, and again when stepping from college to a first job, when standing at the altar to become a wife, and again when bending over the cradle of the first babe, when summoned to public office in church or state—each new step should be characterized by a definite waiting on God, that there may be a fresh enduement of power, a recharging of the spirit with His might.

THE CHARACTERISTICS OF DAVID'S REIGN IN HEBRON

For seven years and six month, David was king in Hebron over the house of Judah. He was in the prime of life, thirty years of age, and seems to have given himself to the full enjoyment of the quiet sanctities of home. Sandwiched between two references to the long war that lasted between his house and that of Saul is the record of his wives and the names of his children (2 Samuel 3:2–5).

Throughout those years, David preserved that same spirit of waiting expectancy that was the habit and temper of his soul and that was so rarely broken in upon. In this he reminds us of our Lord, who sits at His Father's side until His foes are made the footstool of His feet. Similarly, David sat on the throne of Judah, in the city of Hebron—meaning fellowship—waiting until God had leveled all difficulties, removed all obstacles, and smoothed the pathway to the supreme dignity that He had promised. The only exception to this policy was David's request that Michal should be restored to him. It would perhaps have been wiser for them both had she been left to the husband who seemed really to love her. But David may have felt it right to insist on his legal status as the son-in-law of the late king and as identified by marriage with the royal house.

With this exception, David maintained an almost passive policy. What fighting was necessary, David left to Joab. The overtures for the transference of the kingdom of Israel were finally made by Abner himself, who for years had known that he was fighting against God. Abner at last told the puppet king whom he had set up and supported that what God had sworn to David he was resolved to effect—namely, to translate the kingdom from Dan even to Beersheba from the house of Saul to that of David. The negotiations with Israel and Benjamin were carried out by Abner in entire independence of David. It was Abner who had communications with the elders of Israel and spoke in the ears of Benjamin and went finally to speak in the ears of David in Hebron all that seemed good to Israel and to the whole house of Benjamin. It was Abner who proposed to David to go and gather all Israel unto him, addressing him as lord and king and bidding him prepare to rule over all that his soul desired (2 Samuel 3:17–21).

Throughout these transactions, David quietly receives what is offered. He asserts himself with intensity and passion on only two occasions: when it was necessary to clear himself of complicity in dastardly crimes and to show his detestation and abhorrence of those who had perpetrated them.

It was a noble spectacle when the king followed the bier of Abner and wept at his grave. David forgot that this man had been his persistent foe, remembering him only as a prince and a great man. David wove a bouquet of elegiacs to lay on Abner's grave, as he had done for Saul's. It is not surprising that all the people took notice of it and that it pleased them, as whatever the king did pleased the people.

Then followed the dastardly assassination of the puppet king, Ish-bosheth. His had been a feeble reign throughout. Located at Mahanaim on the eastern side of Jordan, he had never exercised more than a nominal sovereignty. All of Ish-bosheth's power was due to Abner, and when Abner was taken away, the entire house of cards crumbled to pieces and the hapless monarch fell under the daggers of traitors. As soon as they bore the tidings to David, bringing Ish-bosheth's head as ghastly evidence, David turned to the Lord, who had redeemed him from all adversity, and solemnly swore that he would require at their hands the blood of the murdered man. The reward for the tidings borne by the Amalekite who asserted he had taken Saul's life was death, and surely nothing less could be the sentence on wicked men who had slain a righteous man in his own house upon his bed.

Then came all the tribes of Israel to Hebron and offered David the crown of the entire kingdom. They remembered his kinship with them as their bone and flesh, recalling his former services when, even in Saul's days, he led out and brought in their armies. And they reminded him of the divine promise that he should be shepherd and prince. Then David made a covenant with them, becoming their constitutional king, and was solemnly anointed for the third time. David was now king over the entire people—as the Son of Man shall be one day acknowledged king over the world of men and shall reign without a rival.

It is to this period that we must attribute Psalm 18, which undoubtedly touches the high-water mark of rapturous thankfulness and adoration. Every precious name for God is acknowledged in helping to bring this to pass. The figure of the Lord coming to rescue His servant in a thunderstorm is unparalleled in sublimity. We can hear the rattle of the hailstones, see the forked lightning flash and the gleam of the coals of fire, but there is throughout an appreciation of the tenderness and love of God's dealings with His children that might have been written by the apostle whom Jesus loved: "Thou hast also given me the shield of thy salvation: and thy right hand hath holden me up, and thy gentleness hath made me great" (v. 35).

20

OH, FOR THE WATER OF THE WELL OF BETHLEHEM!

Let us be patient, God has taken from us
The earthly treasures upon which we leaned,
That from the fleeting things that lie around us
Our clinging hearts should be for ever weaned.

Anna L. Waring

*I*t must have been a rare and imposing assembly that came to crown David king of all Israel. The Chronicles record the names and numbers of the principal contingents that were present on that memorable occasion (1 Chronicles 12:23, etc.).

Mighty men of valor from Judah and Simeon; Levites, led by Jehoiada and Zadok; famous men from Ephraim; men of Issachar who had understanding of the times; of Zebulun, such as were not of double heart and could order the battle array. These and many more came with a perfect heart to Hebron to make David king over all Israel. For three days they remained with him, keeping a great festival, the provisions being contributed by such distant tribes as

133

Zebulun and Naphtali as well as by those near at hand so that all Israel participated in the joy of the occasion.

The Philistines, however, were watching the scene with profound dissatisfaction. So long as David was content to rule as a petty king in Hebron, leaving them free to raid the northern tribes at their will, they were not disposed to interfere. But when they heard that they had anointed David king over all Israel, all the Philistines went down to seek David. They probably waited until the august ceremonial was over and the thousands of Israel had dispersed to their homes, and then they poured over into Judah in such vast numbers—spreading themselves in the Valley of Ephraim and cutting off David's connection with the northern tribes—that David was forced to retire with his mighty men and faithful six hundred to the hold, which, by comparison of passages, must have been the celebrated fortress cave of Adullam (2 Samuel 5.17; 23:13–14).

A Sudden Reversal Of Fortune

It was only a day before that David was the center of the greatest assembly of warriors that his land had seen for many generations. With national acclaim, David had been carried to the throne of a united people. He realized that he was fondly enshrined in the hearts of his countrymen. But today David is driven from Hebron—where for more than seven years he had dwelt in undisturbed security—back to that desolate mountain fastness, in which years before he had taken refuge from the hatred of Saul. It was a startling reversal of fortune, a sudden overcasting of a radiant noon, a bolt out of a clear sky. It is probable, however, that David took refuge in God. These were days when he walked very closely with his Almighty Friend, and he did not for a moment waver in his confidence that God would perfect What concerned him, establishing him firmly in his kingdom.

Such sudden reversals come to us all—weaning us from confidence in men and things, keeping us from building our nest on any earth-grown tree, and forcing us to root ourselves in God alone. It was salutary that David should be reminded at this crisis of his history that he was as dependent on God as ever and that He who had given could as easily take back His gifts. Child of mortality, such lessons will inevitably be set before you to learn. In the hour of most radiant triumphs, you must remember Him who has considered you fit to be His steward. You must understand that your place and power are yours only as His gift and as a trusteeship for His glory. Be not surprised, then, if He makes your throne tremble now and again, that you may remember that it rests, not on some inherent necessity, but only on the determination of His will and the forth-putting of His might.

This contrast between the anointing of Hebron and the conflict of Adullam presents a striking analogy to the experiences of our Lord, who, after His anointing at the banks of the Jordan, was driven by the Spirit into the wilderness of Judea to be forty days tempted of the devil. It is the law of the spiritual life. The bright light of popularity is too strong and searching for the perfect development of the divine life. Loneliness, solitude, temptation, conflict—these are the flames that burn the divine colors into our characters. These are the processes through which the blessings of our anointing are made available for the poor, the broken-hearted, the prisoners, the captives, and the blind.

GLEAMS OF LIGHT

The misty gloom of these dark hours was lit by some notable incidents. The mighty men excelled themselves in single combats with the Philistine champions. It was then that Abishai, the son of Zeruiah, smote the giant, who with his new sword thought to have slain David; and Elhanan slew the brother of Goliath of Gath; and Jonathan, David's nephew, slew a huge monstrosity who had defied Israel; and Eleazar stood in the breach, when the rest had fled, and smote the Philistines until his hand was weary and the disconcerted soldiers returned only to spoil. Such prodigies of valor were performed around the person of their Prince, whom his followers delighted to call the Light of Israel, albeit for the hour obscured by clinging mists (2 Samuel 11:17).

What marvels may be wrought by the inspiration of a single life! We cannot but recall the hour when an unknown youth stepped forth from the affrighted hosts of Israel to face the dreaded Goliath. Alone, so far as human support went, he had encountered and defeated that terrible antagonist. But now, after some fourteen or fifteen years had run their course, David no longer stood by himself. There were scores of men, animated by his spirit, inspired by his faith, who pushed him gently back and told him that they must be permitted to bear the brunt of the conflict, since his life, which was the fountain source of all their energy, must be carefully withheld from needless peril.

Thus the lives of great men light up and inspire other lives. They mold their contemporaries. The inspiration of a Wesley's career raises a great army of preachers. The enthusiasm of a Carey, a Livingstone, a Paton stirs multitudes of hearts with missionary zeal. Those who had been the disciples of Jesus became His apostles and martyrs. Jesus' own life of self-sacrifice for men has become the lighthouse that has summoned myriads from the lowland valley of selfishness to the surrender, the self-denial, the anguish of the Cross, if only they might be permitted to follow in His steps.

A Touching Incident

Adullam was not far from Bethlehem. Often, in his earliest years, David had led his father's flocks to pasture amid the valleys where he was now sheltering. The familiar scenes recalled, as a scent or strain is likely to do, memories that came trooping back from the past and spoke to him of Jesse, his mother, and his boyhood home.

One sultry afternoon, as it would seem, these recollections were unusually fresh and vivid. David was a semiprisoner in the hold. Over yonder, almost within sight, a garrison of Philistines held Bethlehem. Suddenly an irresistible longing swept across him to taste the water of the well of Bethlehem that was by the gate. Almost involuntarily, David gave expression to the wish. He did not suspect that any of his stalwarts were within earshot or, if they were, that they would be foolhardy enough to attempt to gratify his whim. If he had thought this, however, he miscalculated. He had not gauged the warmth of the affection with which those strong men loved him.

Three of his mightiest warriors overheard their chieftain's wish, stole secretly out of the cave and down the valley, burst through the host of the Philistines, drew water from the well, and, before they had been missed, placed the brimming vessel in David's hands. It was the priceless expression of a love that was stronger than death. He could not drink it. To him the vessel seemed gleaming crimson with the blood it might have cost. With the instinctive chivalry of soul that made him in all the changes of his fortune so absolutely kingly as to compel the enthusiastic devotion of his adherents, David arose and poured it out as a sacrifice to God, as though the gift were fit only to be made to Him. David said, as he did so, "Be it far from me, O LORD, that I should do this: is not this the blood of the men that went in jeopardy of their lives?" (2 Samuel 23:17).

We have another example in this graphic episode of David's marvelous self-control. Up to this time, David seems to have never allowed a desire to have unchallenged sway. The wayward impulse of passion and the assertion of a whim were repressed by the iron determination of the purpose in all things to live according to the loftiest ideals of manhood and kingliness. The question of self-gratification was always secondary to the considerations of high and noble principle.

It is good for us to ask ourselves whether certain gratifications that we have been accustomed to indulge are not purchased at too dear a cost. Would we drink a cup of pleasure in the theater if we realized that it was presented to our lips at the cost of scores of souls whose modesty and virtue were being sacrificed behind the scenes? Could we drink of the intoxicating beverage if we realized that the drinking customs of society were annually costing the happiness, the life, and the eternal welfare of myriads?

How often we sigh for the waters of the well of Bethlehem! We go back on our past and dwell longingly on never-to-be-forgotten memories. Oh, to see again that face, to feel the touch of that gentle hand, to hear that voice! Oh, to be again as in those guileless happy years when the forbidden fruit had never been tasted and the flaming sword had never been passed! Oh, for that fresh vision of life, that devotion to the Savior's service, that new glad outburst of love! Oh, that one would give us a drink of the water from the well of Bethlehem! They are vain regrets when there are no mighties strong enough to break through the serried ranks of the years and fetch back the past. But the quest of the soul may yet be satisfied by what awaits it in Him who said, "Whosoever drinketh of this water shall thirst again: But whosoever drinketh of the water that I shall give him shall never thirst; but the water that I shall give him shall be in him a well of water springing up into everlasting life" (John 4:13–14). Not in Bethlehem's well, but in Him who was born there, shall the soul's thirst be quenched forever.

THE OVERTHROW OF THE PHILISTINES

Prosperity had not altered the attitude of David's soul in its persistent waiting on God. As he was when first he came to Hebron, so he was still. In this hour of perplexity, he inquired of the Lord, saying, "Shall I go up to the Philistines? wilt thou deliver them into mine hand?" (2 Samuel 5:19). In reply, David received the divine assurance of certain victory, and when the battle commenced, it seemed to him as if the Lord Himself were sweeping them before Him like a winter flood that rushes down the mountainside, carrying all before it in its impetuous rush. "The LORD," said David, "hath broken forth upon mine enemies" (2 Samuel 5:20). The routed foe had no time even to gather up their gods, who fell into the conqueror's hands.

Again the Philistines came up to assert their olden supremacy, and again David waited on the Lord for direction. It was good that he did so because the plan of campaign was not as before. Those who rely on God's cooperation must be careful to be in constant touch with Him. The aid that was given yesterday in one form will be given tomorrow in another. In the first battle, the position of the Philistines was carried by assault; in the second, it was turned by ambush. To have reversed the order or to have acted on the two occasions identically would have missed the method and movement of those divine legions who acted as David's invincible allies.

This movement in the mulberry trees, indicating that the ambush must rise and attack the foe, suggests the footfalls of invisible angelic squadrons passing onward to the battle. "For then shall the LORD go out before thee, to smite the host of the Philistines" (2 Samuel 5:24). Then David broke on their ranks and pursued them from Gibeon down into the heart of the maritime plain.

Sometimes we have to march, sometimes to halt. At one moment we are called to action, the next to suffering. In this battle, we are to rush forward like a torrent; in the next, to glide stealthily to ambush and wait. We must admit nothing stereotyped in our methods. What worked well in the house of Dorcas will not suit the stately palace of Cornelius. Let there be living faith in God, the calm waiting on the housetop in prayer, the perception of the new departure that the Spirit of God is intending and foreshadowing, and the willingness to follow, though it be at the sacrifice of all the older prejudices. Then shall we know what God can do as a mighty cooperating force in our lives, making a breach in our foes and marching His swift-stepping legions to our aid.

21

2 Samuel 5

JERUSALEM, THE HOLY CITY

Fair Jerusalem,
The Holy City, lifted high her towers.

Milton,
Paradise Regained

One of the first acts of the new king was to secure a suitable capital for his kingdom. His choice of Jerusalem was a masterpiece of policy and statesmanship. Surely, it was more—it was the result of the direct guidance of the Spirit of God. This was the time of which Jehovah speaks in that passage of Ezekiel: "I passed by thee, and looked upon thee, behold, thy time was the time of love;... yea, I sware unto thee, and entered into a covenant with thee, saith the LORD God, and thou becamest mine" (16:8).

It was highly desirable that the capital should be accessible to the whole country and should possess the necessary features that rendered it fit to become the heart and brain of the national life. It must be capable of being strongly fortified so as to preserve the sacred treasures of the kingdom. It must combine features of strength and beauty so as to arouse the national pride and devotion. It must be hallowed by sacred associations so as to become the religious center of the people's holiest life. All these features blended in Jerusalem and commended it to David's divinely guided judgment. In this David greatly differed from Saul, who had made his own city, Gibeah, his capital—an altogether insignificant place and the scene of an atrocious crime, the infamy of which could not be obliterated. To have made Hebron the capital would have excited the jealousy of the rest of Israel, and Bethlehem, his birthplace, would have struck too low a keynote. None were to be compared with the site of Jerusalem, on the frontier between Judah and Benjamin, surrounded on three sides by valleys and on the other side, the north, strongly fortified.

ITS PREVIOUS HISTORY

To the Jew there was no city like Jerusalem. It was the city of his God, located in his holy mountain: "Beautiful for situation, the joy of the whole earth" (Psalm 48:2). The high hills of Bashan were represented as jealous of the lowlier hill of Zion because God had chosen it for His abode. The mountains that stood around her seemed to symbolize the environing presence of Jehovah. The exile in his banishment opened his windows toward Jerusalem as he knelt in prayer and wished that his right hand might forget its cunning sooner than his heart fail to prefer Jerusalem above its chief joy. The charm of the yearly pilgrimage to the sacred feasts was that the feet of the pilgrim should stand within her gates. And when at a distance from her walls and palaces, pious hearts were accustomed to praying that peace and prosperity might be within them for the sake of those brethren and companions who were favored to live within her precincts. The noblest bosom that ever throbbed with true human emotion heaved with convulsive sobs at the thought of the desolation impending over her. Jesus wept when He beheld the city and said: "0 Jerusalem, Jerusalem,...how often would I have gathered thy children together, even as a hen gathereth her chickens under her wings, and ye would not!" (Matthew 23:37).

But it had not always been so. Her birth and nativity were of the land of the Canaanite. An Amorite was her father, and her mother a Hittite. In the day that Jerusalem was born, she was cast out as a deserted child on the open field, weltering in her blood. For a brief spell, the priest-king Melchizedek reigned over her, and during his life, her future glory must have been presaged: the thin spiral columns of smoke that arose from his altars, anticipating the stately worship of the temple; his priesthood foreshadowing a long succession of priests. Thereafter, a long spell of darkness befell her, and for years after the rest of the country was in occupation of Israel, Jerusalem was still held by the Jebusites. Joshua, indeed, nominally subdued the city in his first occupation of the land and slew its king, but his tenure of it was very brief and slight. The city quickly relapsed under the sway of its ancient occupants.

THE CAPTURE

Making a levy of all Israel, David went up to Jerusalem. For the first time in seven years, he took the lead of his army in person. Passive when he was called to wait for the gift of God, he was intensely active and energetic when he discerned the divine summons. The Jebusites ridiculed the attempt to dislodge them. They had held the fortress for so long and were so confident of its impregnable walls that in derision they placed along the walls a number of cripples, boasting that they would be strong enough to keep David and his whole army at bay. But it appears from the narrative given by Josephus that Joab, incited by David's proclamation of making the captor of the city his commander-in-chief, broke in by a subterranean passage, excavated in the soft limestone rock, made his way into the very heart of the citadel, and opened the gates to the entire army.

Whether this story is true or not, it is certain that through Joab's prowess the city speedily fell into David's hands, and David dwelt in the stronghold, afterward known as Zion, or the City of David. This was only part of what was afterward known as Jerusalem. Moriah, where the temple was later erected, was probably an unoccupied site. Araunah, the Jebusite, had a threshing floor there.

David's first act was to extend the fortifications. "And David built round about from Millo and inward" (2 Samuel 5:9), while Joab seems to have repaired and beautified the buildings in the city itself. This first success laid the foundation of David's greatness. "And David went on, and grew great, and the Lord God of hosts was with him" (2 Samuel 5:10). Indeed, neighboring nations appear to have become impressed with the growing strength of his kingdom and hastened to seek his alliance (1 Chronicles 11:7–9; 2 Samuel 5:11).

A Fair Dawn

It has been suggested that we owe Psalm 101 to this hour in David's life. David finds himself suddenly called to conduct the internal administration of a great nation that had, so to speak, been born in a day and was beginning to throb with the intensity of a long-suspended animation. The new needs were demanding new expression. Departments of law and justice, of finance, and of military organization were rapidly being called into existence and becoming localized at the capital. Functionaries and officials of every description were being created. The palace and court were every day thronged with those who sought promotion to offices of trust. It was highly desirable that no mistake should be made in these early selections and that the country could be reassured as to the character of the men whom the king was prepared to entrust with its concerns. For these purposes, this psalm may have been prepared. In any case, it exactly suits such an occasion and purpose.

The royal psalmist declares in Psalm 101 that he will behave himself wisely in a perfect way and will walk within his house with a perfect heart. He will set no base things before his eyes and hate the work of those who turn aside. Then he describes those who shall be his chosen counselors and ministers. He will listen to no privy slanders, subtly suggested to his ear, as from another Doeg or Cush. He will not suffer Hamans, with their high looks and proud hearts, to rule his council and oppress the poor Mordecais at the gate. If he discovers deceit or falsehood in any of his attendants, any species of deception or misrepresentation, he pledges himself to dismiss them instantly. His earliest and best energies should be devoted to cutting off all workers of iniquity from the city of the Lord and to the destruction of all the wicked of the land. Meanwhile, David's eyes should be upon all the faithful of the land, *they* should dwell with him, and he would choose as his most favored attendants those who walked in a perfect way.

It was a beautiful ideal. These early days of the new kingdom were fitly described by him as he reviewed them from the threshold of eternity, as a morning without clouds or as when the tender grass springs out of the earth through clear shining after rain. The conception of the righteous ruler, ruling men in the fear of God and thrusting away the ungodly as thorns and briars, stood out sharply defined and clear-cut before him. It beckoned him to follow, and if only David had obeyed and followed, without swerving to the right or left, what tears of blood, what years of anguish would have been saved! As a dying man, that ideal of more than thirty years came back on him and compared sadly with what had actually befallen him. It was bitter to contrast what had been with what might have been. The muddy swamp in which the river of his life had nearly lost itself bore little resemblance to the clear crystal of its first inception (2 Samuel 23:1–5).

22

2 Samuel 6

THE BRINGING OF THE ARK TO MOUNT ZION

Hark! what a sound, and too divine for hearing,
Stirs on the earth, and trembles in the air!
Is it the thunder of the Lord's appearing?
Is it the music of His people's prayer?
Surely He cometh! and a thousand voices
Shout to the saints, and to the deaf are dumb!
Surely He cometh! and the earth rejoices,
Glad in His coming, who hath sworn, "I come."

F.W. Myers

*A*s soon as David had acquired a capital, he was eager to make it the spiritual as well as the political center of the national life. With this object in view, he resolved to place in a temporary structure close to his palace the almost forgotten ark. Since its return from the land of the Philistines, the ark had found a temporary resting place in the "city of the woods," some eleven miles southwest of Jerusalem, in the house and under the care of Abinadab.

In all probability, David felt unable to remove the tabernacle, which, after Saul's slaughter of the priests, had been set up in the high place that was at Gibeon, because Zadok the priest and his brethren the priests ministered to it and maintained the burnt offering continually upon the altar. An old root of jealousy lay between the families of Zadok and Abiathar, and it was wiser in every way not to bring them together or to interfere with the religious rites that had been maintained through the broken years of recent history (1 Chronicles 16:39, etc.). But David's purpose would be sufficiently served by securing the presence of the ark in the heart of the new city. David would not, however, take any step upon his own initiative but consulted with the captains of thousands and of hundreds, even with every leader. With their acquiescence, David sent abroad everywhere throughout all the land of Israel to gather priests, Levites, and people to bring again the sacred emblem.

THE MISTAKE OF THE CART

It was a great procession that wended its way that day to the little town. In addition to a vast host of priests and Levites and a great gathering of people, there were thirty thousand chosen soldiers, whose presence would be sufficient to protect the assembly from any hostile incursion or surprise.

Probably we owe Psalm 132 to this occasion. The royal singer records the determination that he had formed in the days of his affliction, that whenever he should be delivered from them and established in his kingdom, one of his earliest acts would be to find out a place for the Lord, a tabernacle for the mighty one of Jacob. Then follow the magnificent stanzas that refer directly to this event:

> Lo, we heard of it in Ephra-tah:
> we found it in the fields of the wood.
> We will go into his tabernacles:
> we will worship at his footstool.
> Arise, O LORD, into thy rest;
> thou, and the ark of thy strength (vv. 6–8).

But one fatal mistake marred the events of the day and postponed the fulfillment of the nation's high hope and resolve. It was strictly ordained in the law of Moses that Levites alone, specially consecrated to the task, should bear the ark upon their shoulders— not touching it with their hands lest they should die (Numbers 4:15; 7:9). Nothing could be clearer than this specific injunction or more obvious than the reason for it, in enforcing the sanctity of all that pertained to the service of the Most High. This command had, however, fallen into disuse with much else, and it was arranged that the ark should be carried on a new cart driven by the two sons of Abinadab. This mistake could not be passed over. That the Philistines had used such a cart with impunity had been permitted because they did it ignorantly, but for Israel to set aside the repeated injunction of the Levitical law and follow their own caprice could not be condoned lest the entire Levitical code should be treated as a dead letter and sink into disuse.

The oxen started amid a blast of song and trumpet, and for the first two miles all went well until they came upon a piece of rough road on which the oxen stumbled and the ark shook so violently as to be in danger of being thrown to the ground. Then Uzzah, the younger son of Abinadab, who perhaps had become too familiar with the sacred emblem, put out his hand to steady it and instantly fell dead. The effect on the procession was terrific. Horror silenced the song, and panic spread through the awed crowd as the tidings of the catastrophe spread backward through its ranks. David was greatly dismayed. He was afraid of God that day and said, "How shall the ark of the LORD come to me?" (2 Samuel 6:9). So he directed that the ark should be deposited in the house of Obed-edom, a Levite who lived in the vicinity, and there it remained for three months. The terrified crowds returned to Jerusalem in consternation and dismay.

It has been suggested in some quarters that the breach of Uzzah was a needlessly severe act of God—a too stern treatment of a sin of ignorance. On the other hand, it must be borne in mind how important it was at this juncture to insist on literal obedience to the ancient code. If it had been permitted to man's caprice to set its injunctions at defiance, it is easy to see that the entire system might have fallen into disuse and its important functions been left unrealized.

THE SHOULDERS OF LIVING MEN

"The LORD blessed Obed-edom and all his household," (2 Samuel 6:11). Josephus states that from the moment the ark rested beneath his roof a tide of golden prosperity set in so that he passed from poverty to wealth—an evident sign that Jehovah had no controversy with those who obeyed the regulations and conditions laid down in the ancient law. In the meantime, David searched into the divine directions for the conveyance of the sacred emblem, for he said: "None ought to carry the ark of God but the Levites: for them hath the LORD chosen to carry the ark of God, and to minister unto him for ever" (1 Chronicles 15:2).

Again a vast multitude was gathered. This time, however, the prescribed ritual was minutely observed. The children of the Levites bore the ark of God upon their shoulders, with the staves thereon, as Moses commanded according to the word of the Lord. Then the deep bass of the white-robed choirs, the clash of the cymbals of brass, the sweet strains of the bands of psalteries and harps, the measured march of the captains over thousands, the stately procession of the elders, the shoutings of the teeming crowds of all Israel— together made up such a welcome as was worthy of the occasion and thrilled the soul of David, responsive as a musical instrument to a master hand. Clad in a linen ephod, David leaped and danced before the Lord (2 Samuel 6:14).

So they brought in the ark of the Lord, setting it in its place in the midst of the tent that David had pitched for it. And David offered burnt offerings and peace offerings before the Lord. Then he turned to bless the people in the name of the Lord of Hosts and distributed to them bread and wine and raisins. The one cloud that marred the gladness of the day was the biting speech of Michal, who had no sympathy with her husband's religion. Poor woman! Perhaps she was jealous of David's independence of her and her father's house. Hence the venom in her speech to the man whom she had loved and whose life she had once saved.

THREE MAJESTIC PSALMS

Upon this occasions, three of David's greatest psalms were composed: 15, 68, and 24. Psalm 15 was evidently composed with direct reference to the death of Uzzah and in answer to the question: "LORD, who shall abide in thy tabernacle? who shall dwell in thy holy hill?" (Psalm 68), which was chanted as a processional hymn, begins with the ancient formula, uttered in the desert march each time the camp was struck: "Let God arise, let his enemies be scattered: let them also that hate him flee before him."

As the ark was borne forward in its majestic progress, the symphony was softly played that told of the ancient days in which God went before His people and marched through the wilderness while the earth trembled and the heavens dropped at His presence.

As the Levite bearers drew near the ascent of the road up to the citadel of Zion, the high mountains of Bashan were depicted as regarding its lowlier height with envy. And then, as the august procession swept up the steep, the choristers broke into a strophe of unrivaled grandeur, the full meaning of which could be fulfilled only in the ascension of the Christ Himself, far above all principality and power into the presence of His Father: "Thou hast ascended on high, thou has led captivity captive: thou hast received gifts for men; yea, for the rebellious also, that the LORD God might dwell among them" (Psalm 68:18).

An enumeration of the constituent parts of that mighty host follows: the singers who went before and the minstrels that followed after, the damsels who played with timbrels and the great host of women publishing the tidings, little Benjamin and the princes of Judah, the princes of Zebulun and of Naphtali. Finally, the psalmist anticipates the gathering of distant nations to that sacred spot: "Princes shall come out of Egypt; Ethiopia shall soon stretch out her hands unto God" (Psalm 68:31).

But Psalm 24 is perhaps the master ode of the three. It begins with a marvelous conception, when we consider the narrowness of ordinary Jewish exclusiveness: "The earth is the LORD's, and the fullness thereof; the world, and they that dwell therein."

The first half of the psalm answers the question as to the kind of men who may stand before with God (vv. 3–6). They must be clean in hands and pure in heart, not lifting their soul to vanity nor swearing deceitfully. No mere ablutions or external ceremonial will meet the case. The requirements of this holy God is the righteousness that He alone can give to those who seek His face.

The second half of the psalm declares God's willingness to abide with man upon the earth. The low-browed gates, beneath which Melchizedek may have come forth to greet Abraham, seemed all too low to admit the ark borne aloft on the Levites' shoulders. The gates were bidden to lift up themselves and open to the entering king. In thunders of voice and instrument, the white-robed choirs, halting before the closed portals, cried: "Lift up your heads, O ye gates; and be ye lift up, ye everlasting doors; and the King of glory shall come in" (Psalm 24:7).

Then, from within, a single voice, as though of some startled and suspicious warder, demands: "Who is this King of glory?" A question that met with the immediate, emphatic, and mighty response: "The LORD strong and mighty, the LORD mighty in battle" (v. 8).

Again the challenge to open. Again the inquiry. Again the magnificent reply, that the King of glory—for whom admittance was demanded to this ancient city, held once by demons, the nest of every unclean bird—is the Lord of Hosts, to whom all angels, all demons, all the living things in heaven and on earth and under the earth are subject. So the ark at last reached its resting place.

23

THAT IT WAS
IN THINE HEART

There lives
A Judge, who, as man claims by merit, gives;
To whose all-pondering mind a noble aim,
Faithfully kept, is as a noble deed;
In whose pure sight all virtue doth succeed.

Wordsworth

With the assistance of Hiram, king of Tyre, a palace of cedar had been erected for David on Mount Zion. It was a remarkable contrast to the shelter of Adullam's cave, or even to any house David might have occupied during his stay at Hebron. It was a great contrast also to the temporary structure that served as a house for the ark. One day the impulse suddenly came to David to realize a purpose, the germ thought of which had probably been long in his heart. Calling Nathan the prophet, now mentioned for the first time, David announced to him his intention of building a house for God. For the moment, the prophet cordially assented to the proposal, but in the quiet of the night, when Nathan was more able to ascertain the thought of God, the word of the Lord came to him and told him to prevent the king from taking further steps in that direction.

The next day Nathan broke the news to David with the utmost delicacy and gentleness. Indeed, in the account of his interview with the king, it is difficult to detect the sentence that contained the direct negative. The impression of the whole is that the offer was refused, but the refusal was wrapped up in so many assurances of blessing, in so much promise and benediction, that the king was hardly cognizant of disappointment amid the rush of intense and overwhelming gladness that Nathan's words aroused: "Shalt thou build me an house for me to dwell in?... He shall build an house for my name" (2 Samuel 7:5, 13).

A CONCEPTION OF A NOBLE PURPOSE

It was a great thought that came to David. It was in part suggested by the pressing needs of the situation. After the ark had come to its new home, Asaph and others had been appointed to celebrate and thank and praise the Lord and minister before Him (1 Chronicles 16:4–37). It is supposed that at this period the twenty-four courses of priests were appointed, an arrangement that lasted to the time of our Lord. It is also supposed that the Levites were now organized—twenty-four thousand to help the priests, four thousand as musicians and singers, four thousand as guards and watchmen, while the remainder were scattered throughout the land to teach the law, execute justice, and perform other public offices. It was an immense body of men who thus gathered around the ark and palace for whom it was necessary to find suitable headquarters. This no doubt partly urged David toward the fulfillment of his purpose. But surely there was a deeper reason—to show his love for God, to establish some monument of his reverence, devotion, and lasting gratitude.

It is thus, especially in young life, that great conceptions visit the soul. Ideals of surpassing beauty cast a light forward upon the future. Resolves of service for God and man brace the soul as the air from the glaciers does the dwellers in the plains. All life assumes a nobler aspect and is set to a higher key. Secretly that young person resolves to be a preacher, missionary, or philanthropist. "I will do this great thing for God," the young heart says to itself, altogether heedless of sacrifice, tears, blood. The bugle note of lofty purpose rings out gladly, summoning the soul to noble exploit, and it is saved from the low levels that satisfy others by the immortal hope that has already gone forward to occupy the future.

Young people, never surrender your ideal or act unworthily of it or disobey the heavenly vision. Above all, when you come as David did to the house of cedar and God has given you rest, be more than ever careful to protect yourselves and to remember the purpose that visited you when you kept your father's sheep.

THE IDEAL IS NOT ALWAYS REALIZED

There is no definite "no" spoken by God's gentle lips. God presses His promises and blessings upon us, leading us forward in a golden haze of love that conceals His negative. Like David, we cannot point out the word or moment of refusal. We are lovingly carried forward from sentence to sentence in life's long speech of divine care and bounty. It is only in moments of review that we find that our purpose is not destined to work itself out just as we thought.

The plant is conscious of a great possibility throbbing within it, but somehow the days pass, and it does not come to a flower. The picture that is to gain immortality is always *to be* painted; the book that is to elucidate the problem of the ages is always *to be* written; the immortal song is always *to be* sung. The young man is kept at his desk in the business place instead of going to the pulpit; the girl becomes an older woman, cherishing a faded flower; the king hands over to his son the building of the house.

GOD EXPLAINS HIS REASONS AFTERWARD

What we know not now we shall know afterward. Years after, David said to Solomon his son, not born at this time, "But the word of the LORD came to me, saying, Thou hast shed blood abundantly, and hast made great wars: thou shalt not build an house unto my name" (1 Chronicles 22:8). The bloodstained hand might not raise the temple of peace. It would have wounded David needlessly to have been told this at the time. It was enough to wrap up the divine no in a promise of infinite blessing, but as the years passed, the reason for God's refusal grew clear and distinct before David. Meanwhile, David possessed his soul in patience and said to himself: *God has a reason. I cannot understand it, but it is good.*

Someday we shall understand that God has a reason in every no that He speaks through the slow movement of life. God would reveal it to us if we could bear it, but it is better not to pry into the mystery of His providence. He fences our questions, saying, "If I will that he tarry till I come, what is that to thee?" (John 21:22). But the time will come, probably in this life—certainly in the next—when the word of the Lord will come to us, and from the eminence of the years we shall catch sight of why He led us as He did.

An Unrealized Dream May Yet Contain An Immense Blessing

Solomon completes the story: "But the LORD said to David my father, Forasmuch as it was in thine heart to build an house for my name, thou didst well in that it was in thine heart" (2 Chronicles 6:8). David was a better man because he had given expression to the noble purpose. Its gleam left a permanent glow on his life. The rejected candidate to the missionary cause stands upon a higher moral platform than those who were never touched by the glow of missionary enthusiasm. For a woman to have loved passionately, even though the dark waters may have engulfed her love before it was consummated, leaves her ever after richer, deeper, than if she had never loved or been loved in return. That a plant should have dreamed in some dark night of the possibility of flowering into matchless beauty stamps it as belonging to a higher family than the moss that clings around the stump. "Thou didst well in that it was in thine heart."

The martyrs in the apocalyptic vision behold a day when their wrongs will be avenged, but they are told to wait, since God's time had not come. In the meanwhile, white robes are given them (Revelation 6:11). Their ideal was not yet, but it purified them and bound them closer to the Christ.

God will credit us with what has been true of our heart. He who has the missionary's heart, though he be tied to an office chair, is reckoned as one of that noble band. The woman at Zarephath, who did nothing more than share her last meal with the prophet, shall have a prophet's reward. The soul that thrills with the loftiest impulses, who the cares of the widowed mother or dependent relatives stay in fulfillment, will be surprised one day to find itself credited with the harvest that would have been reaped had those seed germs been cast on more propitious soil. In the glory, David will find himself credited with the building of the temple on Mount Zion.

Do The Next Thing

The energy that David would have expended in building the temple wrought itself out in gathering the materials for its construction. "I have prepared with all my might for the house of my God..." (1 Chronicles 29:2, etc.). If you cannot have what you hoped for, do not sit down in despair and allow the energies of your life to run to waste. Arise and strengthen yourself to help others to achieve. If you may not build, you may gather materials for him who shall. If you may not go down the mine, you can hold the ropes.

There is a fact in nature known as the law of the conservation of force. The force of the accumulating velocity of the falling stone passes into heat, of which some is retained by the stone and the rest passes into the atmosphere. No true ideals are fruitless; somehow they help the world of men. No tears are wept, no prayers uttered, no conceptions honestly entertained in vain.

Somehow God makes up to us. He stooped over David's life in blessing. The promise made through Nathan was threefold: (1) that David's house should reign forever, (2) that David's seed should build the temple, and (3) that the kingdom of Israel should be made secure. As we read the glowing words, we feel that they could be realized only in Him whom Peter declares David foresaw. There is only One of the sons of men whose reign can be permanent, and His kingdom without end, who can bring rest to the weary sons of men and build the true temple of God (Acts 2:30). But how great the honor that He should be David's Son!

Then David the king went in and sat before the Lord, and he said, "Who am I, O Lord God..." (2 Samuel 7:18). We have no words to characterize the exuberant outflow of his soul in that transcendent hour. There was no complaint that the purpose of his heart was thwarted amid the successive billows of glory that swept over his soul. Does God withhold the less and not give the greater? Does He refuse the offer we make and not bestow some heavenly gift that enriches forevermore? Dare to trust Him. Sit before Him and let His assurances comfort you. Claim that He should do as He has said and know that not one good thing shall fail. "For brass I will bring gold, and for iron I will bring silver, and for wood brass, and for stones iron:... The sun shall be no more thy light by day; neither for brightness shall the moon give light unto thee: but the LORD shall be unto thee an everlasting light, and thy God thy glory" (Isaiah 60:17, 19).

24

2 Samuel 8; 1 Chronicles 18–20

YET HAVE
I SET MY KING

Crown Him the Lord of Heaven!
Enthroned in worlds above;
Crown Him the King to whom is given
The wondrous name of Love,
Crown Him with many crowns,
As thrones before Him fall:
Crown Him, ye kings, with many crowns,
For He is King of all!

Godfrey Thring

*T*he time of rest that followed the removal of the ark was broken in upon by a succession of fierce wars. One after another, the surrounding nations gathered together, either singly or in confederacies, against David. "The heathen raged, the kingdoms were moved" (Psalm 46:6).

The Philistines. For the last time, the Philistines arose, but David smote and subdued them and, to use the significant phrase of the Revised Version, took the bridle of the mother city out of their hand.

The Moabites. The hereditary alliance, dating from the time of Ruth, between the Hebrew monarch and his restless neighbors was insufficient to restrain them. Benaiah was commissioned to lead an expedition against them that was so successful that their entire

159

army fell into his hands and was dealt with according to the terrible custom of the time, one third only being spared.

The Syrians. The king of Zobah and the Syrians of Damascus were utterly defeated. Vast spoils of gold and brass fell into David's hand, and the border of Israel was carried to the line of the Euphrates so that the ancient promise made by God to Abraham was fulfilled: "Unto thy seed have I given this land, from the river of Egypt unto the great river, the river Euphrates" (Genesis 15:18).

Edom. While David was engaged in the north, the Edomites invaded Judah, and Abishai was dispatched against them. On the west shore of the Dead Sea, David encountered them and slew eighteen thousand in the valley of Salt. The whole land, even to Petra, its rock-bound capital, was slowly reduced to submission. With the exception of Hadad, who made his way to Egypt, the royal family of Edom was exterminated.

Ammon. A friendly overture on the part of David was met with gross insult, and Hanun, apprehending the infliction of merited revenge, formed a vast coalition. The combined forces amounted to thirty-two thousand, with a strong contingent of cavalry and chariots, against which David could only oppose the Hebrew infantry, the use of horses being forbidden by the Mosaic legislation. It was a supreme moment in David's career and taxed the utmost resources of Joab's generalship. By God's good hand, however, victory was secured. The tide of Israelite invasion swept over the hostile country, and Rabbah, the capital city, fell into David's hand. The people were put to work with saws, arrows, and axes, probably preparing the materials for the erection of public works and perhaps of the temple itself.

These years of war gave birth to some of the grandest of the psalms, among which may be numbered Psalms 2, 20, 21, 60, and 110.

THE FOE

The nations rage, and the people imagine a vain thing. "The kings of the earth set themselves, and the rulers take counsel togethers against the LORD, and against his anointed, saying, Let us break their bands asunder, and cast away their cords from us" (Psalm 2:1–3)

They trust in chariots and in horses. Their kings think that they will be saved by the multitude of their hosts. They inspire fear through the hearts of Israel so that the land trembles as though God had rent it, and the people drink the wine of staggering and dismay. So tremendous is their assault, so overwhelming their numbers, that all help of man seems vain.

It is thus in the era of the history of God's people that Satan has stirred up their foes. Right behind the coalition of men lies the malignity of the fallen spirit, whoever seeks to bruise the heel of the woman's seed. "In the world ye shall have tribulation" (John 16:33). "Behold, the devil shall cast some of you into prison, that ye may be tried; and ye shall have tribulation ten days" (Revelation 2:10). "And when the dragon saw that he was cast unto the earth, he persecuted the woman" (Revelation 12:13).

THE ATTITUDE OF FAITH

While the serried ranks of the foe are in sight, the hero king is permitted a vision into the unseen and eternal. There is no fear upon the face of God, no change in His determination to set His king upon His holy hill. In fact, it seems that the day of David's foe's attack is that in which David receives a new assurance of sonship, and David is told to claim the nations for his inheritance and the uttermost parts of the earth for his possessions. As he anticipates the battle, David hears the chime of the divine promise above the tumult of his fear: "Thou shalt break them with a rod of iron; thou shalt dash them in pieces like a potter's vessel" (Psalm 2:9).

On David's leaving the capital, his people pray that the Lord may answer him in the day of trouble, remember his offerings, and send him help from the sanctuary, and David replies: "Now know I that the LORD saveth his anointed; he will hear him from his holy heaven with the saving strength of his right hand" (Psalm 20:6). David knows that through the lovingkindness of the Most High he shall not be moved but that His right hand will destroy his enemies.

In the ecstacy of his faith, David asserts, as he looks eastward across the Jordan, that Gilead will as certainly own his sway as Ephraim and Manasseh did. Strong in the allegiance of Judah and her sister tribes, he counts victory already secured. Moab is his washing basin; Edom like a slave shall carry his shoes; Philistia shall tremble before his war shout; and even the strong city of Petra shall receive his troops.

In perfect peace David anticipates the result. The Lord will send forth the rod of His strength out of Zion and strike through kings in the day of His wrath, making His enemies His footstool so that in all afterdays He may combine the office of priest and king, as Melchizedek did on that same site centuries before (Psalm 110).

The Warriors Of The Priest King

Catching the contagion of David's faith, the king's warriors triumph in God's salvation and in His name set up their banners. They believe that God, as a Man of War, is going forth with their hosts and will tread down their adversaries. They are characterized by the *willingness of their service.* No mercenaries are pressed into their ranks. They gladly gather around the standard as the warriors of whom Deborah sang, who willingly offered themselves.

They are clad not in armor, but in the fine linen of the priests. "The beauties of holiness" (Psalm 110:3), a phrase that suggests that the warfare was conducted by religious men, was an act of worship to God.

They are numerous as the dewdrops that adorn the morning grass when every blade has its own coronet of jewels and the light is reflected from a million diamonds.

What an exquisite conception of David's ideal for his soldiers—of the knightly chivalry, of the purity, truth, and righteousness, in which all the soldiers of the Messiah should be arrayed!

The Completeness Of The Victory

The armies of the foreigner cannot stand the onset of those heaven-equipped soldiers. Kings of armies flee quickly. They are bowed down and fallen in bitter, hopeless defeat. They are made as a fiery furnace in the time of God's anger and swallowed up in His wrath. Their dead bodies strew the battlefield, and the valleys are choked with slain.

As the triumphant army returns, leaving desolation where their foes had swarmed, they express in song their gratitude to their Almighty Deliverer. Singers and minstrels, Benjamin and Judah, Zebulun and Naphtali, join in the mighty anthem in Psalm 68:

> He that is our God is the God of salvation;
> and unto God the Lord belong the issues from death....

O God, thou art terrible out of thy holy places:
the God of Israel is he that giveth strength and power unto his
people (v. 20, 35).

All this has a further reference. In David we have a type of the
Messiah. For, of a truth, against the Holy Servant Jesus, whom God
has anointed, both the Gentiles and the peoples of Israel have
gathered together. Men have refused His sway and do refuse it, but
God has sworn and will not repent that to Him every knee shall
bow and every tongue confess. It is more sure than that tomorrow's sun will rise that before long, great voices shall be heard in
heaven, saying, "The kingdoms of this world are become the kingdoms of our Lord, and of his Christ; and he shall reign for ever and
ever" (Revelation 11:15).

25

2 Samuel 11–19

THE SIN
OF HIS LIFE

O Father, I have sinned! I have done
The thing I thought I never more should do!
My days were set before me, light all through;
But I have made dark—alas, too true!—
and drawn dense clouds between me and my Sun.

Septimus Sutton

*T*he book of Chronicles omits all reference to this terrible blot on David's life. The older record sets down each item without extenuation or excuse. The gain for all penitents would so much outweigh the loss to the credit of the man after God's own heart. These chapters have been of immeasurable worth to the myriads who, having nearly lost themselves in the same dark labyrinth of sin, have discovered the glimmer of light by which the soul may pass back into the day: "Her sins, which are many, are forgiven;... go in peace" (Luke 7:47, 50).

THE CIRCUMSTANCES
THAT LED TO DAVID'S SIN

The warm poetic temperament of the king especially exposed

him to a temptation of this sort. But the habit of self-restraint in his life would have prevailed had there not been some slackening of commitments.

For seventeen years David had enjoyed an unbroken spell of prosperity. In every way he had been successful, on every great occasion increasing the adulation of his subjects. This was fraught with peril. The rigors of the Alps are less to be dreaded than the heat of the listless plains of the Campagna.

In direct violation of the law of Moses—which forbade the multiplication of wives on the part of Hebrew kings, lest their hearts should turn away (Deuteronomy 17:17)—we are distinctly told that when established at Jerusalem, David took more concubines and wives. He sowed to himself the inevitable harvest of heart burning, jealousy, quarreling, and crime, of which the harem must always be the prolific source, besides fostering in David himself a habit of sensual indulgence that predisposed him to the evil solicitation of that evening hour.

David had also yielded to a time of indolence, unlike the martial spirit of the Lion of Judah. Allowing Joab and his brave soldiers to do the fighting around the walls of Rabbah, David remained at Jerusalem. It was a mood to which Uriah administered a stinging rebuke when he refused to go to his own house while his comrades and the ark were encamped on the open field.

One sultry afternoon, the king had risen from his afternoon nap and was lounging on his palace roof. In that hour of ease, to adopt Nathan's phrase, a traveler came to a rich man, and to render hospitality, the rich man descended into the home of a poor man and took his one ewe lamb, although the rich man's own folds were filled with flocks. We will not extenuate his sin by dwelling on Bathsheba's willing complicity while she despised her marriage vows to her absent husband. The Scripture record lays the burden of the sin on the king alone, before whose absolute power Bath-sheba may have felt herself obliged to yield.

One brief spell of passionate indulgence, and then!—David's character blasted irretrievably, his peace vanished, the foundations of his kingdom imperiled, the Lord displeased, and great occasion given to his enemies to blaspheme! Let us beware of our light, unguarded hours. Moments of leisure are more to be dreaded than those of strenuous toil. Midlife—for David was above fifty years of age—has no immunity from temptations and perils that beset the young. One false step taken in the declension of spiritual vigor may ruin a reputation built up by years of faithful exercise.

A message came one day to David from his companion in sin that the results of their liaison could not be hidden. It made his blood run with hot fever. The law of Moses punished adultery with the death of each of the guilty pair. Instant steps must be taken to veil the sin! Uriah must come home! He came, but his coming did not help the matter. He refused to go to his home, though on the first night the king sent him a special meat straight from his table and on the second made him drunk. The chivalrous soul of the soldier shrank even from sexual relations with his wife while the great war was still in process.

There was no alternative but that Uriah should die, for dead men tell no tales. If a child was to be born, Uriah's lips, at least, should not be able to disown it. Uriah bore to Joab, all unwitting, the letter that was his own death warrant. Joab must have laughed to himself when he got it. "This master of mine can sing psalms with the best. But when he wants a piece of dirty work done, he must come to me. He wants to rid himself of Uriah—I wonder why? Well, I'll help him to it. At any rate, he will not be able to say another word to me about Abner. I shall be able to do as I will. He will be in my power from now on."

Uriah was set in the forefront of the hottest battle and left to die. The significant item of his death was inserted in the bulletin sent to the king from the camp. It was supposed by David that only he and Joab knew of this thing, and it was probable that Bath-sheba did not guess the costly method by which her character was being protected. Bath-sheba lamented for her dead husband, as was the custom of a Hebrew matron, congratulating herself meanwhile on the fortunate coincidence, and within seven days she was taken into David's house. A great relief this! The child would be born under the cover of wedlock! There was one fatal flaw, however, in the whole arrangement: "But the thing that David had done displeased the LORD" (2 Samuel 11:27). David and the world were to hear more of it. But oh, the bitter sorrow, that he who had spoken of walking in his house with a perfect heart, with all his desires for divine fellowship, with all the splendid record of his life behind him, should have fallen thus! The psalmist, the king, the man, the lover of God, all trampled in the mire by one dark, wild, passionate outburst. Ah, me! My God, grant that I may finish my course without such a rent, such a blot! Oh, to wear the white flower of a blameless life to the end!

DELAYED REPENTANCE

The better the man, the dearer the price he pays for a short season of sinful pleasure. For twelve whole months, the royal sinner wrapped his sin in his bosom, pursed his lips, and refused to confess. But in Psalm 32, David tells us how he felt. His bones waxed old through his roaring all the day long. He was parched with fever heat, as when in Israel for three years there was neither dew nor rain in answer to Elijah's prayer, and every green thing withered in the awful drought of summer. Day and night God's hand lay heavily upon him.

When David took Rabbah, he treated the people with ferocious cruelty, as if he was weary of his own remorse, expending on others the hardness that he ought to have dealt out to himself. We often excuse ourselves from avenging our own sin by our harsh behavior and uncharitable judgments toward others. The same spirit that always characterizes the sullen, uneasy conscience flamed out in his sentence on the rich man who had taken the poor man's lamb (2 Samuel 12:5). The Levitical law in such a case only adjudged fourfold restoration (Exodus 22:1). The king pronounced a sentence of death.

Nathan's advent on the scene must have been a positive relief. One day while statesmen and soldiers were crowding the outer corridor of the cedar palace, the prophet, by right of an old acquaintance, made his way through them and sought a private audience. He told what seemed to be a real and moving story of high-handed wrong, and David's anger was greatly kindled against the man who had perpetrated it. Then, as a flash of lightning on a dark night suddenly reveals to the traveler the precipice and the void of which he is about to place his foot, the brief, awful stunning sentence, "Thou art the man!" (2 Samuel 12:7) revealed David to himself in the mirror of his own judgment and brought him to his knees. Nathan reminded David of the past and dwelt specially on the unstinted goodness of God. It was a sunny background, the somber hues of which made recent events look the darker: "Wherefore hast thou despised the commandment of the LORD...thou hast killed Uriah...and hast taken his wife...I will take thy wives before thine eyes...the child also that is born unto thee shall surely die" (2 Samuel 12:9, 11, 14). "I have sinned against the LORD," was David's only answer—a confession followed by a flood of hot tears—and instantly his scorched heart found relief (2 Samuel 12:13). Oh, blessed showers that visit parched souls and parched lands!

When Nathan had gone, David beat out that brief confession into Psalm 51, dedicated to the chief musician, that all the world might use it, setting it to music if they would. The one sin and the many transgressions, the evil done against God as though even Uriah might not be named in the same breath, the confession of inbred evil, the ache of the broken bones, the consciousness of the unclean heart, the loss of joy, the fear of losing the Holy Spirit, the broken and contrite heart—thus the surcharged waters of the inner lake broke forth muddled and dark. Ah, those cries for the multitude of God's tender mercies! Nothing less could erase the dark legend from the book of remembrance or rub out the stains from his robe or make the leprous flesh sweet and whole. To be clean because purged with hyssop, to be whiter than snow because washed, to sing aloud once more because delivered from blood-guiltiness, to be infilled with a steadfast, a willing, and a holy spirit, to be able to point transgressors to the Father's heart—these were the petitions that his weak, sin-weary heart laid upon the altar of God, sweeter than burnt offering or fragrant incense.

But long before this prayer of brokenness was uttered, immediately on his acknowledgment of sin, without the interposition of a moment's interval between his confession and the assurance, Nathan had said, "The LORD hath put away thy sin" (2 Samuel 12:13).

> I acknowledged my sin unto thee, and mine iniquity
> have I not hid.
> I said, I will confess my transgressions Unto the LORD,
> and thou forgavest the iniquity of my sin (Psalm 32:5).

Penitent soul! Dare to believe in the instantaneous forgiveness of sins. You have only to utter the confession to find it interrupted with the outbreak of the Father's love. As soon as the words of penitence leave your lips, they are met by the hurrying assurances of a love that, while it hates sin, has never ceased to yearn over the prodigal.

Sin is dark, dangerous, damnable, but it cannot staunch the love of God. It cannot change the love that is not of yesterday but dates from eternity itself. The only thing that can really hurt the soul is to keep its confession locked within itself. If only with stuttering, broken utterance it dares to cry, "Be merciful to me, the sinner, for the sake of the blood of Jesus that was shed," it instantly becomes white as snow on Alpine peaks or as pure as the waters of mid-ocean that the stain of the great city cannot soil or as transparent as the blue sky that is the curtain of the tabernacle of the Most High.

26

2 Samuel 12–19

THE STRIPES OF THE CHILDREN OF MEN

No action, whether foul or fair,
Is ever done, but it leaves somewhere
A record written by fingers ghostly,
As a blessing or a curse, and mostly
In the greater weakness or greater strength
Of the acts which follow it.

Longfellow

Sin may be forgiven, as David's was, and yet a long train of sad consequences ensue. The law of cause and effect will follow on, with its linked chain of disaster. But God's mercy to His erring and repentant children will be shown in converting the results of their sin into the fires of their purification, in setting alleviation of the tenderest sort against their afflictions, and in finally preventing the further outworking of evil. All these facts stand out upon the pages that tell the story of God's chastisement, alleviations, and deliverances.

O soul of man, this is solemn reading for us. It is the inner story of God's dealing with His own. As He dealt with David, He will deal with us. He will forgive, but He may have to use the rod. He may restore to His favor and yet permit us to drink the bitter waters that our sin has tapped. Be meek, patient, and submissive. You will come forth out of the ordeal a purified soul, and others shall learn through your experiences the goodness and severity of God. Forgiven men may have to reap as they have sown.

GOD'S CHASTISEMENTS

Bath-sheba's little child was very sick. It was the child of sin and shame, but the parents hung over it. For seven days, the mother watched it and the father fasted and lay on the earth. David suffered more in seeing the anguish of the babe than if ten times its pain had been inflicted on himself. It cuts to the deepest when the innocent suffer for our crimes. On the seventh day the child died (2 Samuel 12:18).

Two years later, one of his sons treated his sister as David had treated Uriah's wife. They say a man never hears his own voice till it comes back to him from a recording. Certainly a man never sees the worst of himself until it reappears in his child. In Amnon's sin David beheld the features of his own unbridled passions. And in Amnon's murder by Absalom two years later, David encountered again his own bloodguiltiness. Absalom's fratricide would never have taken place had David taken instant measures to punish Amnon. But how could he allot that penalty to his son's impurity that he had evaded for himself (Leviticus 18:9–29)? Nor could David punish Absalom for murder when he remembered that he, a murderer, had eluded the murderer's fate.

When presently Absalom's rebellion broke out, it received the immediate sanction and adherence of David's most trusted councillor whose advice was like the oracle of God. What swept Ahithophel into the ranks of that great conspiracy? The reason is given in the genealogical tables that show that he was the grandfather of Bath-sheba and that his son Eliam was the comrade and friend of Uriah.

It is thought by some that at this time David was smitten with some severe form of disease. Psalms 41 and 60 are supposed to record his sufferings during these dreary years. They tell the tale of his depression, depict the visitors that surrounded his bed, and recount the comments they passed on the sick man.

The most disastrous and terrible blow of all was the rebellion of Absalom, whose handsome features, ready wit, apparent sympathy with the anxieties and disappointments of the people fretting under the slow administration of the law, his sumptuous expenditure and splendor had for four years been undermining David's throne and stealing sway the hearts of the people. When Absalom erected his standard at Hebron and was proclaimed king throughout the land, it was evident that the people had lost their former reverence and love for David—perhaps the story of his sin had disappointed and alienated them—and they hurried to pay their homage at the shrine of the new prince.

We need not recount the successive steps of those stormy days: the panic-stricken flight of the king, "Arise, and let us flee... make speed to depart"(2 Samuel 15:14), the barefoot ascent of Olivet, the anguish that wept with loud voice, the shameful cursing of Shimei, the apparent treachery of Mephibosheth, the humiliation of David's wives in the sight of the sun that had witnessed his own sin, the gathering of all Israel together unto Absalom in apparent oblivion of the ties that for so many years had bound them to himself.

Such were the strokes of the father's rod that fell thick and fast upon his child. They appeared to emanate from the malignity and hate of man, but David looked into their very heart and knew that the cup that they held to his lips had been mixed by heaven and was not the punishment of a Judge but was the chastisement of a Father.

Outside the story of Christ there is nothing in the Bible more beautiful than David's behavior as he passed through this tangled growth of thorns. "Carry back the ark of God," David said to Zadok; "he will bring me again, and shew me both it, and his habitation: But if he thus say, I have no delight in thee; behold, here am I, let him do to me as seemeth good unto him"(2 Samuel 15:25–26). And when Shimei—perhaps referring to the recent execution of the sons of Rizpah and perhaps suggesting that he had been guilty of the death of Ishbosheth—called him a man of blood because of his dealings with Saul's house, David said to Abishai, "The LORD hath said unto him, Curse David. Who shall then say, Wherefore hast thou done so?"(2 Samuel 16:10). Thus, when Judas brought the bitter cup to the lips of Christ, the Master said, "The cup which my Father hath given me, shall I not drink it?"(John 18:11). Let us never forget the lesson. Pain and sorrow may be devised against us by the malignity of an Ahithophel, a Shimei, or a Judas. But if God permits such things to reach us, by the time they have passed through the thin wire of His sieve, they have become His will for us. We may look up into His face and know that we are not the happening of chance or wild misfortune or human caprice but are being trained as sons. Without such chastisement we might fear that we were not His children.

GOD'S ALLEVIATIONS

The trials came in many ways. The bitter hour of trial revealed a love on the part of his adherents of which the old king may have become a little oblivious.

Ahithophel's defection cut David to the heart. David tells the story in the psalms we have mentioned. His sensitive nature winced to think that the man of his friendship, in whom he trusted and who did eat of his bread, had lifted up his heel against him. But then Hushai the Archite came to meet him with every sign of grief and was willing, as his friend, to plead in the council chamber of Absalom.

Shimei might curse him, but Ittai the stranger, a man of Gath, with all his men, swore allegiance for life or death.

Zadok and Abiathar are there with the ark, their ancient animosity forgotten in their common sorrow for their master. Ziba meets him with summer fruits, clusters of raisins, and loaves of bread. Shobi and Machir and Barzillai make abundant provision for his hungry, weary, and thirsty followers. David's people tell him that he must not enter the battle, because his life is priceless and worth ten thousand of theirs.

It was as though God stooped over that stricken soul and as the blows of the rod cut long furrows in the sufferer's back, the balm of Gilead was poured into the gaping wounds. Voices spoke more gently, hands touched his more softly, pitiful compassion rained tender assurances about his path, and—better than all—the bright-harnessed angels of God's protection encamped about his path and his lying down.

Thus he came to sing some of his sweetest songs, among them Psalms 3, 4, 61, 62, 63, and 143. The two former are David's morning and evening hymns, when his cedar palace was exchanged for the blue canopy of the sky. David knows that he has many adversaries who say, "There is no help for him in God"(Psalm 3:2). But he reckons that he is well guarded: "But thou, O LORD, art a shield for me; my glory, and the lifter up of mine head"(Psalm 3:3).

David is not afraid of ten thousands of the people. He lies down in peace to sleep and awakes in safety because the Lord sustains him. He knows that the Lord has set him apart for Himself and feels that the light of His face will put more gladness into his heart than the treasures of the kingdom that he seemed to have forfeited forever.

Then, from the drought-stricken land that they were obliged to traverse, his soul thirsts to see the power and glory of God as he had seen them in the sanctuary, and already he realizes perfect satisfaction. To long for God is to find Him, and to thirst after Him is to feel the ice-cold water flowing over the parched lips. With these came a clear prevision of the issue of the terrible strife: "The king shall rejoice in God; every one that sweareth by him shall glory: but the mouth of them that speak lies shall be stopped"(Psalm 63:11).

GOD'S DELIVERANCE

The new troops that Absalom had so hastily mustered were unable to stand the shock of David's veterans, and they fled. Absalom himself was killed by the ruthless Joab as he swayed from the arms of the huge terebinth. The pendulum of the people's loyalty swung back to its old allegiance, and the people eagerly contended for the honor of bringing the king back. Even the men of Judah, conscious of having forfeited David's confidence by so readily following Absalom, repented and urged him to return. Shimei cringed at his feet. Mephibosheth established his unfaltering loyalty. Barzillai was bound to the royal house forever by his profuse acknowledgments and the royal offers to Chimham. All seemed ending well.

One unfortunate occurrence delayed the peaceful conclusion of the whole matter. The ten tribes were greatly irritated that Judah had made and carried through all the arrangements for the king's return, and they gave vent to hot, exasperating words. These the men of Judah answered with equal heat. At an inopportune moment, Sheba shouted the trumpet of sedition and raised the cry that was destined in the days of Rehoboam again to rend the land, "Every man to his tents, O Israel"(2 Samuel 20:1). The ten tribes immediately receded, and another formidable revolt arose at David's feet and was only put down by incredible exertions on the part of Joab. The death of Sheba was the last episode in this rebellion that was quelled in blood and always left a scar and seam in the national life.

Many were the afflictions of God's servant, but out of them all David was delivered. When he had learned the lesson, the rod was put away. David had been chastened with the rod of men and with the stripes of the children of men, but God did not take away His mercy from David as from Saul. David's house, his throne, and his kingdom, in spite of many conflicting forces, were made sure. The rod, the stripes, and the chastisements are always true, but amid all these, the love of God, carrying out His redemptive purpose, never hasting, never resting, never forgetting, but making all things work together till the evil is eliminated and the soul purged. Then the afterglow of blessing, the calm ending of the life in a serene sundown.

27

1 Chronicles 20–29

SUNSET AND EVENING STAR

Sunset and evening star,
And one clear call for me,
And may there be no moaning of the bar
When I put out to sea!

Tennyson

A period of ten years of comparative repose was granted David between the final quelling of the revolts of Absalom and Sheba and his death. The recorded incidents of those years are few. It is probable that David walked softly and humbly with God, not paying attention to high things but concentrating his attention on the building of the temple, which had been the dream of his life. If he might not build it himself, he would strive with all his might to help him who would.

ITS SITE

The site of the temple was indicated in the following manner. David conceived the design of numbering Israel and Judah. The Book of Chronicles says that Satan moved David to the site, while the older record attributes the suggestion to the anger of the Lord. It is not impossible to reconcile these two statements, since the Old Testament writers so frequently attribute to God's agency what we would refer to His permissive Providence.

The sin of numbering the people probably lay in its motive. David was animated by a spirit of pride and vain glory. He was eager to make a fine showing among the surrounding nations and impress them with such a conception of Israel's greatness that they might not dare to attack any point on the long frontier line. There was a tendency to exchange his chosen position of waiting only on God and trusting in the arm of human prowess and organization.

In spite of the protests of Joab and others, the king persisted, sending the officers to and fro throughout the land to take the sum of the people. Truly the nation had grown vastly, since it was a scattered, demoralized remnant after the defeat of Gilboa. Excluding the tribes of Levi and Benjamin and the city of Jerusalem, the fighting men of Israel numbered about a million, and those of Judah five hundred thousand.

When the enumeration was nearly complete and the officers had reached Jerusalem, David's heart smote him, and he said to the Lord: "I have sinned greatly, because I have done this thing" (1 Chronicles 21:8). David saw how far he had swerved from the idea of the theocracy, in which God's sovereignty alone determined the nation's policy. He had substituted his own whim for the divine edict, involving himself and his people in the charge of emulating the kings and nations around. A night of anguish could not, however, wipe out the wrong and folly of nine months. David might be forgiven but must submit to one of three modes of chastisement. It was wise on his part to choose to fall into the hands of God, but the plague that devastated his people with unparalleled severity cut him to the quick.

Sweeping through the country, the plague came at last like a destroying army to the holy city, and it seemed as if the angel of the Lord were hovering over it, sword in hand, to begin His terrible commission. Then it was that David cried unto the Lord, pleading that His judgments might be stopped: "Is it not I that commanded the people to be numbered? even I it is that have sinned and done evil indeed; but as for these sheep, what have they done?" (1 Chronicles 21:17). And the angel of the Lord stayed by the threshing floor of Ornan the Jebusite, who is thought by some to have been the deposed king of the old Jebusite city. There, on Mount Moriah, where centuries before the angel had stayed the uplifted knife of Abraham, God said, "It is enough, stay now thine hand" (1 Chronicles 21:15). That spot became the site of the temple. At the direction of the prophet Gad, David purchased the threshing floor, the threshing instruments, and the oxen that trod out the grain. He insisted on paying the full price, that he might not give God that which cost him nothing. And from then on, Mount Moriah became the center of national worship, the site of successive temples, and the place of the manifestation of the Son of Man.

ITS BUILDER

The last year of David's life, and the fortieth of his reign, was embittered by a final revolt of the discordant elements that had so often given David trouble. Joab at last turned traitor to his old master, and Abiathar, instigated probably by jealousy of Zadok, joined him in espousing the cause of Adonijah, the eldest surviving son. They must have known God's distinct assurance that Solomon was His chosen king, but they realized that there was little hope of being entrusted with his confidence and therefore resolved on making one last effort to set him aside and deliver to the nation a nominee of their own.

When the account of the revolt was brought to David, it stirred the old lion heart, and though he had reached the extreme point of physical exhaustion, he aroused himself with a flash of his former energy to take measures for the execution of the divine will communicated to him years before: "And the king sware, and said, As the LORD liveth, that hath redeemed my soul out of all distress, Even as I sware unto thee,...even so will I certainly do" (1 Kings 1:29-30). Not many hours passed before tidings broke in on Adonijah's feast at Enrogel, saying that Solomon had been anointed king in Gihon by the hand of Zadok the priest and Nathan the prophet and had ridden through the city on the royal mule, escorted by Benaiah and his men-at-arms. Within an hour, the whole of Adonijah's supporters had melted away, and he was clinging, as a fugitive, to the horns of the altar.

It was probably about this time that David gave Solomon the charge to build the house for God. He recounted the steps by which he had been led—from his desire to build the house and the divine refusal on account of his having shed so much blood, to the divine assurance that a son should be born who would be a man of rest and could build the Temple of Peace. David then enumerated the treasures he had accumulated and the preparatory works that had already been established. It is almost impossible for us to realize the immense weight of precious metal, the unlimited provision of brass, iron, and timber, or the armies of workmen. The surrounding countries had been drained of their wealth and stores to make that house exceedingly magnificent.

At the close of this solemn charge, David added instruction to direct Solomon in his behavior towards Joab and Shimei. It has the appearance of vindictiveness, but we must give the dying monarch credit for being animated with a single purpose for the peace of the realm. Had vengeance been in his heart, David could have taken care of it previously.

Its Pattern

The Jewish state required that the king should not only be anointed by the priest but also recognized by the entire people. It was therefore necessary that David's choice should be ratified in a popular assembly that gathered at the royal command (1 Chronicles 28:1). What an august spectacle must that have been when for the last time the aged king stood face to face with the men who had helped to make Israel great, many of whom had followed him from comparative obscurity! It resembled the farewell of Moses to the people whom he had led to the threshold of Canaan or of Samuel's parting address. For the last time, monarch and people stood together before God. Again David recited the circumstances of his choice, of his desire to build the temple, and the substitution of Solomon for himself. Then turning to the young man who stood beside him, David bade him be strong and carry out the divine purpose.

Next followed the gift of the pattern of all the house that had been communicated to David by the Spirit of God and an inventory of the treasures from which each article was to be constructed. As Moses saw the land of promise gleam before his dying gaze, so to David's imagination the splendid temple stood forth in every part complete. The contribution from his private fortune had been most munificent, and with this as his plea, David turned to the vast crowd, asking princes and people to fill their hands with gifts. The response was splendid. It is probable that never before or since has such a contribution been made at one time for religious purposes. But best of all, the gifts were made willingly and gladly.

With a full heart, David blessed the Lord before all the congregation. His lips were touched with the olden fire. His thoughts expanded beneath the warmth of his imagination and rose to heaven. David ascribed to Jehovah the universal kingdom and recognized that all that had been contributed that day had been first received. Standing upon the threshold of the other world, David's days seemed as a shadow in which there was no abiding. And then the king and father pleaded for Solomon that he might keep the divine statutes and build the house. Last of all, he turned to the people and asked them to join in ascriptions of praise, and there went forth a mighty shout of jubilation, of blessing and praise, while a great religious festival crowned the proceedings.

It was a worthy conclusion to a great life! How long after David lingered, we cannot tell. The sacred historians do not expend their words in describing dying scenes. One record says simply that "David slept with his fathers, and was buried in the city of David" (1 Kings 2:10). Another records that "he died in a good old age, full of days, riches, and honor" (1 Chronicles 29:28). But perhaps the noblest is that uttered by the Holy Spirit through the lips of Paul: "David, after he had served his own generation by the will of God, fell on sleep,...and saw corruption" (Acts 13:36).

It is beautiful to find that word *sleep* used of David's death. David's life had been full of tumult, storm, and passion, of war and blood. Many a revolt had cast its foam in his face, but rest came at last, as it will come to all. Like a tired infant's, those aged eyes closed in the last sleep, and the spirit joined the mighty dead. David's sepulcher remained to the day of Pentecost, for Peter refers to it. But the man whom God had raised up was drinking of the river of His pleasures and became satisfied as he awoke in His likeness. The fairest dreams of his Lord that had ever visited his soul fell short of the reality, and upon David's aged face must have rested in death a look of glad surprise, as though the half had not been told.

The parallel between him and our Lord may be carried into minute particulars. In their anointing, their inimitable words, their sufferings, their zeal for the House of God, their love for their friends, their betrayal by those they had trusted, their wars, their love for Jerusalem—how much in common! But there the parallel stops. In His atoning death, in His incorruptible nature, in His glorious ascension, the Son of David stands alone. David himself, in the Spirit, called Him Lord and knew that Jesus alone could fulfill that ideal of kingship that had passed before his inspired thought, given to Him by the Holy Ghost but that no mere mortal would ever be able to realize.

> He shall come down like rain upon the mown grass:
> as showers that water the earth....
> He shall have dominion also from sea to sea,
> and from the river unto the ends of the earth....
> For he shall deliver the needy when he crieth;
> the poor also, and him that hath no helper....
> his name shall be continued as long as the sun:
> and men shall be blessed in him (Psalm 72:6, 8, 12, 17).